# SACRED MEALS

*From our Family Table*

by

John David Finley

Library of Congress Control Number: 2005926399

ISBN 0-9768430-0-5

First printing. 3000 copies. July 2005

Additional copies of this book may be purchased online at
www.sacredmeals.com

Copies may also be purchased by phone by calling
1-800-573-9337 (toll free)

Published by John David Finley

The Nativity of Christ, The Theophany, The Prophet King
David, The Harrowing of Hell and the Wedding of Cana
used by permission of Holy Transfiguration Monastery,
Brookline, MA.

Painting on Cover
*Still Life with Fish* by Lev Lominago
Copyright 2005 The Lominago Group
*To read more about the extraordinary life of artist/iconographer
Lev Lominago (b. July 17, 1944 d. October 28, 1999)
visit www.lominago.com*

Manufactured under the direction of Double Eagle Industries.
For manufacturing details, call 888-824-4344
or e-mail to info@publishingquest.com

# Table of Contents

## ACKNOWLEDGEMENTS

### GENERAL EDITORS
Janet M. Finley
V. Rev. Peter Gillquist
Frances Roberts
Abbess Victoria

### FOOD AND WINE EDITORS
Janet Benner
Patrick Coffield
Monika Raygoza Finley
Rouba Haddad Heckenlively
John Paise

### FAMILY HISTORY EDITORS
Howard Paul Finley
Owen Clark Finley

### TYPOGRAPHY, COVER AND BOOK DESIGN
Lucy Brown

### COPY EDITOR
Diane Eagle Kataoka

# Table of Measurements for Recipes

**ABBREVIATIONS**

| | | |
|---|---|---|
| 1tsp | = | one teaspoon |
| 1Tbl | = | one tablespoon |
| 1floz | = | one fluid ounce |
| 1c | = | one cup |
| 1pt | = | one pint |
| 1qt | = | one quart |
| 1gal | = | one gallon |
| 1oz | = | one ounce |
| 1lb | = | one pound |
| 1pkg | = | one package |

**CONVERSION CHART**

| | | | |
|---|---|---|---|
| 1tsp | = | | = 5ml |
| 3tsp | = | 1T | = 15ml |
| 2Tbl | = | 1floz | = 30ml |
| 4Tbl | = | 1/4c | = 59ml |
| 5Tbl+1tsp | = | 1/3c | = 79ml |
| 1c | = | 8 fl oz | = 237ml |
| 2c | = | 1pt (16fl oz) | = 473ml |
| 2pt | = | 1qt (32fl oz) | = 946ml |
| 4qt | = | 1gal (128fl oz) | = 3.79l |
| 1lb | = | 16oz | = 454g |

When you don't have fresh herbs and spices use the chart below to make appropriate substitutions.

**EQUIVALENCY CHART**

1Tbl fresh chopped = 1tsp dried = 1/2tsp powdered

**OVEN TEMPERATURE CONVERSION**

Fahrenheit / Celsius

| Fahrenheit | Celsius |
|---|---|
| 225 | 110 |
| 250 | 130 |
| 275 | 140 |
| 300 | 150 |
| 325 | 170 |
| 350 | 180 |
| 375 | 190 |
| 400 | 200 |
| 425 | 220 |
| 450 | 230 |
| 485 | 240 |

# Dedication

*And he shall go before him in the spirit and power of Elijah, to turn the hearts of the fathers to the children, and the disobedient to the wisdom of the just; to make ready a people prepared for the Lord.*[1]

dedicated to our three children
Owen Jefferson III, Holly Marie and John Charles
to our daughter-in-law Monika
and our granddaughter Atalia Isabel

In these pages, my memories of your great grandparents, your grandparents and your mother are brought to life through the wonderful meals we used to share, and still do. But that sharing is more than a sentimental, emotional thing. It is, for me, an entrance into the dimension of the heavenly kingdom, the Eschaton.[2]

All of life is sacramental, that is, something more than what we see or experience or feel on the surface. There is something more, something deeper: memory, fellowship, communion with God. Where do we learn this? How can we experience this higher plane, this hidden mystery?

It begins in Church, where the mystery has been revealed. It begins at the Lord's Table, the heavenly banquet. And it extends into our homes and into every aspect of our lives, when we decide to accept and enter into that greater reality. We can actually take

[1] Luke 1:17
[2] A Greek word meaning "The Age to Come."

that experience of the Kingdom, the light and the life we have received, and communicate it to the world. Our family dinner table at home can become a reflection of the Lord's Table. We remember the events of the day, we have fellowship together, and we look forward to tomorrow as we celebrate our common union.

Some may say that the life described in these pages is nothing more than a description of the life of the 1950s and '60s that formed my childhood memories. You know, however, that despite all the challenges of our family life—the fast pace, the work schedules, the school activities—we struggled to make the life described a reality in our home.

My prayer for you is that you will enter into that same struggle as you move into your adult years, that you will feel in your heart, see with your mind's eye and read in this family cookbook  my love for you, your mother, your grandparents and great grandparents. Most of all, I pray that you will enter into that greater struggle to consistently draw near with the fear of God, with faith and love, to taste the heavenly bread and the cup of life. May you live to see and experience the promise of the good things to come in the everlasting day of the Kingdom.


Dad

# Prayers at the Table

*Man is a hungry being. But he is hungry for God. Behind all hunger of our life is God. All desire is finally a desire for Him. To be sure, man is not the only hungry being. All that exists lives by "eating." The whole creation depends on food. But the unique position of man in the universe is that he alone is to bless God for the food and the life he receives from Him. He alone is to respond to God's blessing with his blessing.[3]*

FR. ALEXANDER SCHMEMANN

It's so easy to "dig in" without pausing to thank God and ask Him to bless the food. In our rush and haste, it seems that we fall short of expressing the fullness of what God created us to be, and in so doing, neglect our sacred calling. This is why it is important for us to say a blessing before we eat.

---

[3] Alexander Schmemann, *For the Life of the World.* (Crestwood, NY: St. Vladimir's Seminary Press, 1973). pp. 14-15.

## Prayers before Meals

*In the Name of the Father, and of the Son, and of the Holy Spirit. Amen.*

*Our Father, Who art in heaven, Hallowed be Thy Name;*
*Thy kingdom come, Thy will be done on earth as it is in heaven.*
*Give us this day our daily bread; and forgive us*
*our trespasses, as we forgive those who trespass against us;*
*and lead us not into temptation,*
*but deliver us from evil.*

*Glory to the Father, and to the Son, and to the Holy Spirit:*
*now and ever and unto ages of ages. Amen.*
*Lord, have mercy. Lord, have mercy. Lord, have mercy.*

then

*O Christ our God, bless the food and drink of Thy servants, for Thou art Holy, always,*
*now and ever and unto ages of ages. Amen.*

or

*They that hunger shall eat and be satisfied, they that seek after the Lord*
*shall praise Him; their hearts shall live forever. Amen.*

or

*Bless us, O Lord, and these Thy gifts of which we are about to partake, for*
*Thou art blessed and glorified; now and ever and unto ages of ages. Amen.*

# Prayers after Meals

*Glory to the Father, and to the Son, and to the Holy Spirit: now and ever and unto ages of ages. Amen. Lord, have mercy. Lord, have mercy. Lord, have mercy.*

then

*Blessed is God, Who is merciful unto us and nourishes us from His bounteous gifts by His grace and compassion, always, now and ever and unto ages of ages. Amen.*

or

*We thank Thee, O Christ our God, that Thou hast satisfied us with Thy earthly gifts, deprive us not of Thy Heavenly Kingdom; but as Thou entered into the midst of Thy disciples, O Savior, and gave them peace, enter also among us and save us. Amen.*

or

*We thank thee, O God, the Giver of all good things, for these gifts and all Thy mercies, and we bless Thy Holy Name, always, now and ever and unto ages of ages. Amen.*

# A Prayer for Thanksgiving Day
## Based on Fr. Alexander Schmemann's Thanksgiving Prayer[4]

*Thank You, O Lord, for accepting our worship of the Holy Trinity, Father,
Son and Holy Spirit, and which filled our hearts with joy, peace, and righteousness.*

*Thank You, O Lord, for having revealed Yourself to us and for giving us the foretaste
of Your Kingdom.*

*Thank You, O Lord, for having united us to one another, in serving You and
Your Holy Church.*

*Thank You, O Lord, for having helped us to overcome all difficulties, tensions, passions,
and temptations and for having restored peace, mutual love and joy in sharing the
communion of the Holy Spirit.*

*Thank You, O Lord, for the sufferings you have bestowed upon us, for they are purifying
us from selfishness and remind us of the "one thing needed: Your eternal Kingdom."*

*Thank You, O Lord, for having given us this country where we are free to
worship You.*

*Thank You, O Lord, for our families, husbands, wives and especially, children,
who teach us how to celebrate Your holy Name with joy.*

*Thank You, O Lord, for the abundance of food and drink of which we are
about to partake.*

*Thank You, O Lord, for everyone and everything. Great are You, O Lord, and
marvelous are Your deeds, and no word is sufficient to celebrate your miracles. Amen.*

[4] Exact text found in "The Orthodox Church," Vol. 20, No. 2, February 1984, p. 1:1.

# CHAPTER 1 ~ *Home for the Holidays*

We used to go down to Ardmore, Oklahoma every year for the Holidays. The drive from McAlester was about two and a half hours. There was always an air of expectancy, for several things, mostly for food!

My grandparents on my mother's side had a big pecan tree in their front yard. Their home was a modest 1920s vintage, single-story house with a full front porch and brick columns. My grandfather, a Spanish-American war veteran and true patriot, usually flew the flag from the front porch on major holidays. My grandmother typically had a bunch of ferns hanging on the porch. By this time of year, though, she had brought them inside, along with her African violets.

My brothers and I would go out to the front yard with our grandfather, climb up into the tree and start rattling the pecans. Pop[5] would pick up a few pecans off the ground, but we didn't get many that way. He would go out in the back to the detached garage, where they parked their '54 DeSoto and grab a couple of long cane poles from the rafters. He would hand them to us and we would start knocking the pecan clusters out of the tree. Soon we would have enough for a couple of my grandmother's pecan pies. It was worth the effort, believe me.

We would come inside and sit around the kitchen table with the tools to extract the pecan meat from the shells. Removing the soft outer hull was no problem, but cracking the hard shell in such a way that we didn't crush the meat inside was a skill to be mastered. I learned through observation, trial and error and eventually got pretty good at it. The objective of course, was to extract the two halves of each pecan completely intact. It didn't make the pies taste better, but it did make them look better.

---

[5] "Pop" was our family nickname for Grandpa Bomar.

## PECAN PIE

3 eggs, slightly beaten
1c brown sugar
1c corn syrup
1/8tsp salt
1/4c melted butter
1c pecans

This recipe is pretty easy. In a medium mixing bowl, combine the eggs, brown sugar, corn syrup, salt and butter. Transfer to an uncooked 9-inch pie shell. Top with intact pecan halves. Bake at 375 for 45-50 minutes.

Perhaps one of the most unique offerings during the Holidays was my grandmother's pear relish. To this day, I've never tasted anything quite like it. As a kid it wasn't my favorite thing, but as an adult, I must say that a turkey dinner without Pear Relish just isn't complete. She had always made it in advance, so I can't remember ever watching her make it, but I learned how, simply by following the recipe and asking my mother for a few tips. My mother says mine is as good as Grandma's.

## PEAR RELISH

1-1/2c vinegar
1-1/2c sugar
1Tbl salt
1Tbl celery seed
1Tbl dried mustard
2tsp allspice
2tsp ground turmeric
1tsp ground ginger
12-16 medium pears, finely chopped (about 4lb)
3 medium onions, diced
2 medium green peppers, diced
1 medium red pepper, diced
4 fresh jalapeño peppers, minced (optional)

Pour the vinegar, sugar and spices into a 6-8 qt. Dutch oven. Finely chop the pears, onions, green peppers and red pepper by hand or in a food processor. Seed the jalapeños and mince. Add to Dutch oven and begin cooking on the stovetop at medium heat. Bring to a boil and cook for 30 minutes. Strain excess juice, then store in an airtight refrigerator container or can in sterilized pint-size Mason Jars.[6] Serve as a side dish with the turkey. Makes about 8 pints.

Of course, cranberries are always a part of any Holiday meal. The Bomar Family tradition was no exception. My grandmother had a special recipe for cranberries; it was a Jell-O Salad and, man, was it good! She would usually set out a small dish of Miracle Whip to top the cranberry salad. My wife Janni says (as politely as she can), "Wow, that's so "not" California!"

## CRANBERRY JELL-O SALAD
1 or 2 Gala or Fuji apples, chopped
1/4c lemon juice
1/4c sugar
12oz package of whole cranberries, chopped
1/2c celery, chopped
11oz can mandarin oranges, drained
1c crushed pineapple, drained
1c pecans, chopped
6oz package of cranberry or orange Jell-O
2c boiling water

Mix apples with lemon juice, and then add sugar, cranberries, celery, mandarin oranges, crushed pineapple and pecans. Prepare Jell-O mixture according to package directions, then pour into the other ingredients. Refrigerate overnight. Top with Miracle Whip if you're from Oklahoma.

[6] Pear Relish should last 1-2 weeks in an airtight refrigerator container. Home canning, however, is my preferred method. Canning should only be done with the proper equipment, clear and reliable instructions, and a very clean environment. Check out www.homecanning.com for proper canning procedures.

Of all the festive drinks in the world, nothing says Christmas to me more than Grandma's Boiled Custard. It's like eggnog, but the store-bought kind has some sort of aftertaste that seems to lose its authenticity once you've tried her B.C.!

## BOILED CUSTARD

6 eggs (separated)
1-1/2c sugar
1/8tsp salt
1Tbl flour
1 can sweetened condensed milk
1Tbl vanilla extract
3/4gal whole milk

Separate eggs and beat whites into soft peaks. Mix egg yolks, sugar, salt and flour. Add condensed milk and stir. Add to a double boiler, then add milk till the double boiler is full. Cook until it coats a wooden spoon. Pour into a one-gallon container. Add vanilla and top it off with milk. Chill. Enjoy with a sprinkle of nutmeg.

This needs a little bit of translation. First of all, I don't usually separate the eggs. I simply break them into a blender and add everything to the blender while heating up the double boiler. I get two large Dutch ovens (one that will fit in the other) making a huge double boiler. When the water starts to boil I add the basic ingredients from the blender (about one quart) and add milk to equal about one gallon.

I cook the mixture in the double boiler until it becomes thick and can coat the back of a spoon. I have to monitor the heat or the eggs in the mixture will curdle. It's done when I don't feel like I'm stirring milk anymore.

Put 1Tbl vanilla into a gallon container then spoon in the boiled custard from the double boiler. Top it off with milk, if needed, and stir to make a full gallon. There is usually a pretty thick layer of custard stuck to the double boiler, which makes for some pretty good eatin'!

## The Main Event

Each year, Christmas Day at our house in Santa Barbara is quite an event. We typically have a number of relatives and a few guests. People always comment on the dressing I make to stuff the turkey. We used to always call it dressing; it seems that most people around here call it "stuffing." Whatever. Mine is made with cornbread and I think that's what surprises most folks; they're used to bread stuffing or the store-bought kind.

Grandma Bomar always made cornbread dressing. I never knew there was any other kind until I was grown. But before I give you her recipe for dressing, you should know that someone else in our family was actually better at fixing cornbread: Grandpa Finley.

I used to watch him put all the ingredients together in a mixing bowl and he would talk to me while he was mixing it up. "John, you have to get the batter just right and it doesn't always turn out following the directions on the package. You have to arrive at a consistency so that when you stir the batter you can see the folds, but when you stop, it goes flat in the bowl." Depending on a multitude of variable conditions, that might mean adding a little buttermilk or adding a little cornmeal; it usually means adding a little buttermilk. Here's the recipe:

## CORNBREAD

*This is a single recipe. Make a double recipe if you're making cornbread for the dressing mix.*

3Tbl canola oil
1-1/3c cornmeal (white or yellow)
2/3c flour
3Tbl sugar
1Tbl baking powder
1tsp salt
1 egg
1-1/3c buttermilk (a little less if using regular milk)

Preheat oven to 400F. Put 1Tbl oil in baking pan and preheat the pan to piping hot! Mix all dry ingredients in a bowl. Add remaining 2Tbl of oil, beaten egg and buttermilk to dry ingredients and combine thoroughly. Bake at 400 for 25 minutes.

When preparing a double recipe for stuffing the turkey, make it the day before so it can be handled easily the next day. Prepare turkey broth before putting the dressing together. Take the giblets and the neck from the turkey, place them in a pan with 5-6c of water, add a little salt and let it simmer for about an hour. Canned chicken broth can be used instead, but you're going to want this giblet broth for gravy later on anyway, so go ahead and fix it.

## CORNBREAD DRESSING (STUFFING)

*Double recipe of cornbread, cooled (about 8 cups)*

1-1/2c celery, chopped
1c onion, diced
1tsp sage (or poultry seasoning)
2c turkey broth (or canned chicken broth)

Slice cornbread into 1/2 inch "crouton" sized cubes and place in a very large mixing bowl. Add chopped celery, diced onion, sage, and mix thoroughly but gently. Finally add the broth a little at a time, being careful not to flood the mixture. This will cause the stuffing to become very "pasty." One technique I use is to pour the broth over a spoon or ladle so as to cause it to rain over the mixture.

The final consistency is somewhat difficult to describe: You want the mixture to break apart when stirred, but "bind" when pressed together. If you use too much broth, it will really gum up on you; too little and you're going to need a lot of gravy at dinnertime.

## SMOKED TURKEY

I always get a 20 lb bird. "Fresh or frozen?" people ask. I once posed the question to my good friend Raegan Amerine, a retired turkey farmer from Oakdale, California. Whenever someone answers a question with a question, I know they know the answer. "When was that fresh turkey killed and prepared for market? You don't know, do you? Frozen turkeys are frozen the same day they are killed and dressed. So, I would recommend frozen if you're getting one from the store."

Grandma Bomar always cooked her bird in the oven. I don't know if she would agree with this or not, but I just love to cook mine on a Weber[7] Grill using the indirect method. If all you've ever cooked on your grill is hamburgers, hot dogs and steaks, you've lived, but you haven't ascended! The taste of a Weber-baked turkey is otherworldly.

When the turkey is ready to be stuffed, and the coals have been started, wash the bird and rub it down with some oil. This is to keep the skin from cracking in the cooking process. Stuff the dressing into both the main cavity and the caboose. The main cavity is usually secured with a metal clip for the legs. Secure the skin at the other end with a small metal skewer. Also, secure the wings to the main cavity with metal skewers to keep them up and away from the direct heat of the coals below the grill.

When the coals are ready, spread them evenly on opposite sides and place a drip pan in the middle. If you do this carefully to keep the drippings away from the ashes, you're going to end up with the most phenomenal turkey gravy you've ever tasted. Center the turkey over the drip pan and place the lid on the grill. Open all the vents fully unless it's quite windy. Grab a cup of coffee, and enjoy the sun and the aromas. Someone who has never celebrated Christmas Day in Southern California may think this sounds nuts. Our climate, however, typically allows for at least the better part of the day to be enjoyed outdoors.

Cook the turkey 13 minutes per pound and restock about 8 coals on each side, every hour. If you've never done this before, the thought of leaving a 20 lb turkey on a BBQ for 4 hr. 20 min. is truly a scary thought! Trust me and trust Mr. Weber; it works beautifully.

---

[7] Specific information on Weber Grills can be found at: http://www.weber.com/bbq/

## The Congregation of Nibblers

There's something about building anticipation in people's minds that's always fun. One thing I like to do is test the cornbread dressing. After the turkey has been on the grill for awhile, it begins to brown on the surface and get crispy. I like to grab someone who looks bored and see if I can perk them up a little bit. I grab a fork, take a little bit of that crispy-brown dressing and hand it to them. The smoke flavor combined with an already outstanding recipe is almost more than anyone can take. "Wow, that's incredible!" is almost always the response.

Test the turkey for doneness more by feel than by temperature. Cut away the dry skin at the leg and thigh from the main cavity and press down slightly on the thigh and leg at the thigh joint. If that joint breaks easily, it's done.

The skin on the bottom side is usually stuck to the grill, but comes loose very easily by just sliding the bird back and forth a couple of times. Carefully lift the bird onto a large butcher block and take it inside, then come back out to get the all-important drip pan from the bottom grate of the grill. The juice from this pan, combined with the remaining turkey stock from the giblets, makes the best smoke-flavored turkey gravy you've ever tasted!

About this time the congregation of nibblers begins to gather in the kitchen. "Do you need any taste testers?" That's my Mother-in-law's line. Whether I do or not, she and others usually volunteer. I don't get irritated. Actually, it's a joy. I like to nibble on the middle section of the wing; it's my favorite part of a BBQ turkey. It almost tastes like bacon.

I like to slice the breast and thigh meat for dinner and save the rest for later. There's something about picking on a cold turkey leg that just can't be beat. You know how the smoke gives the meat that kind of triple coloration: a dark purple surface, a pink under-layer and the gray meat? The leg is really the best, if you like to pick on that kind of meat.

## A Little Attention to Detail

Somehow, the whole process from start to finish is a type of journey: from thinking about it, to making the preparations, to the actual cooking, carving and eating. I always think about Grandma and Grandpa Bomar during the Holidays. Their life is such an inspiration to me. Love— that's really what I think about the most. I knew they loved me, my brothers and my Mom and Dad.

I find myself with the eyes of my heart returning each year to a place that was filled with the love of God, a place of faith that had been sorely tested through life. As I said earlier, Pop was a Spanish-American War Veteran. So great was his patriotism that he actually forged his father's and uncle's signatures in order to sign up with the Tennessee Volunteers!

He thought if he could get to Cuba, perhaps he could become one of Teddy Roosevelt's Rough Riders. Unfortunately, the ship that took the 4th Tennessee Volunteer Infantry ran aground about 20 miles off the southern coast of Cuba, and they were brought to safety in Trinidad on sailboats and barges. After about four months of guarding Cuban plantations, building roads and teaching the locals how to farm, they returned, only to be quarantined out of concern over the spread of yellow fever. Then, in a little over a month, the troops were discharged and they went home.

This quiet man with a great spirit of adventure was once asked by brother Owen why he wanted to go to Cuba. Pop chuckled and said, "I guess I just wanted to be wild and woolly."

He moved to Oklahoma while it was still Indian Territory and worked in Ardmore as a pharmacist into his early 80s. My mother once told me about the time Pop filled a prescription for a lady whose son was sick. After she left the drugstore, he reviewed the prescription and came to the conclusion that the doctor had made a serious mistake. He called the doctor and told him how the prescription was filled and felt it was too high a dose of medicine. The doctor thanked him and immediately called the patient's mother and told her not to give her son the medicine. The mistake was so severe, it would have killed the little boy. Just a little attention to detail saved a life.

Pop liked to whittle wood and carve things. He carved a cane, little boxes and all kinds of stuff. There was a nice tool shed in the garage where he worked. They had a push mower. I can remember going down there during the summertime and watching him mow the grass with that push mower. When he got tired he had me take over. It was much harder work than gliding along with our electric mower at home. I asked him once why he didn't get an electric mower or a gas mower. He said he didn't like the noise. Pop was a man of few words.

There was an old pendulum wall clock that hung on the wall of the den just above the floor furnace. I can see him now, carefully opening the glass compartment so as not to knock the clock off balance. Reaching into the shelf he takes the

*Irving Clark Bomar*
*my maternal grandfather*
*b. Dec 8, 1878 d. Jan 3, 1971*

*Rejoice in the Lord always: and again I say, Rejoice. Let your moderation be known unto all men. The Lord is at hand. Be careful for nothing; but in everything by prayer and supplication with thanksgiving let your request be made known unto God. And the peace of God, which passeth all understanding, shall keep your hearts and minds through Christ Jesus. Finally, brethren, whatsoever things are true, whatsoever things are honest, whatsoever things are just, whatsoever things are pure, whatsoever things are lovely, whatsoever things are of good report, if there be any virtue, and if there be any praise, think on these things.* [8]

---

[8] Philippians 4:4-8. This passage was read at Pop's funeral conducted by Richard T. Hopper, Pastor of the First Baptist Church in Ardmore, Oklahoma. Dr. Hopper directed the passage to the three grandsons: Owen Clark, John David and Howard Paul Finley as an exhortation that he felt our grandfather would have given us at his departure from this life. This exact passage is read as the Epistle Lesson in our Church every Palm Sunday. I always think of Pop on Palm Sunday and take that opportunity with palm branch in hand to renew my commitment to the everlasting Kingdom of God.

key and winds it up a few turns, returns the key to the shelf and carefully closes it. Somehow time stands still as I return to that old clock now mounted on the wall in our dining room, sand think about his life, his faithfulness to God, his family and his country.

I mentioned the old white and green '54 DeSoto Coronado. Grandma always drove and Pop enjoyed the ride, whether it be to church or work or maybe to the cemetery to visit Uncle Clark's grave. Uncle Clark was my mother's older brother who died of cancer in 1944 at the age of 27. Pop would bring the push mower, Grandma the grass shears and flowers. As the scriptures say, even in death, nothing could separate them from the love of their son and the love of God. Such precious memories.

Pop loved ice cream. We always had ice cream on Sunday evening before going to the evening service at the First Baptist Church. He had a hand-held malt machine that made the best milk shakes. He was such a slow eater and took such small bites. Maybe that's one reason why he lived to be 92 years old. Pop was often quoted as saying, "Old age has its joys."

Although he didn't cook much, I can remember watching him cook sausage. He liked J.C. Potter's Country Style Sausage. I could eat a patty in about two or three bites. He would take out his knife and fork and stretch it out to at least 8 or 10 bites. Maybe it was self-restraint; more than likely it was simply his way of celebrating life.

# CHAPTER 2 ~ *Christ is Born! Glorify Him!*

My Grandma and Grandpa Finley lived in McAlester, Oklahoma, just a mile from our house. The streets running north and south in our neighborhoods were numbered and the streets running east and west were named for Indian tribes. They lived on East Seneca. Their house was built in 1919, so it was much like the Bomar house in Ardmore. Their corner lot had a slope, so there was a big rock wall in the front yard. Around the side, the rock wall gradually got smaller and the back of the house was right at ground level.

We always entered through the back door. The breakfast table was right there, with the kitchen to the left and the den to the right. It wasn't just a house, it was a home. Everything was nice and neat, but it was comfortable. We were always at ease. My brothers and I used to fight over who would get to spend the night at their house on Friday nights. Daddy established a rotation system to keep the peace.

*Finley grandparents home in McAlester, Oklahoma*

They had a big attic fan in the hallway and during the summertime they would open a couple of windows and turn on the fan with a wall-mounted timer to create circulation throughout the house. It really worked. The bathroom fixtures were the old-style freestanding tubs with porcelain handles on the sinks.

When I was really small, I used to hide in the compartments of the window seats in the dining room. Maybe it was some kind of "death fixation" or like being in a coffin. I would see how long I could stay in there until I burst open the lid to make sure I was still alive.

The front porch was expansive. Sometimes we would go out there after dinner and just sit and talk, and watch cars and people go by. Life was slow, secure and predictable.

Being a great quail hunter, Grandpa's annual goal was to collect enough quail for Christmas Dinner. Hunting season began in early November. I can never remember a time when we didn't have more than enough for the big feed.

## SMOTHERED QUAIL

12 quail, thoroughly cleaned and halved
3/4c butter[9]
1/4c flour
2-1/2c chicken broth
1/2c sherry (or heavy cream)
salt and pepper to taste

In a skillet, brown quail in melted butter, then transfer to a baking dish. Stir flour into skillet, mixing well. Slowly add chicken broth and sherry (or heavy cream). Salt and pepper to taste. When well blended, pour over quail. Cover and bake at 350F about an hour. Makes 12 servings.

## MASHED POTATOES

8 medium boiling potatoes (about 2lb)
1/2c butter (1 stick)
1Tbl minced garlic (optional)
1c buttermilk (or half-and-half)
salt to taste

Peel and quarter the potatoes, then add to a large pot and cover with water. Bring to a boil and cook until the potatoes are tender when pierced with a fork (15-20 minutes). Drain the potatoes and mash with a potato ricer. Blend in butter, (minced garlic) and buttermilk. Season with salt and serve with gravy from smothered quail.

We had all the other usual trimmings, peas, cranberry sauce and rolls... What I remember most though were my grandmother's desserts. One in particular, her date pudding, was outstanding.

---

[9] If you are preparing fewer quail, just use 1T butter per bird.

## DATE PUDDING

16oz pitted whole dates, finely chopped
3 eggs
1c sugar
1c pecans
1tsp baking powder (make that 1 heaping tsp)
2Tbl flour
a pinch of salt

Preheat oven to 300F. Chop the dates really fine, and set them aside. Separate the egg whites and yokes and reserve both. Beat the egg whites with a mixer to medium peaks. In a medium mixing bowl combine the yolks and the sugar. Add the chopped dates together with the remaining ingredients and mix thoroughly.

Carefully fold in the egg whites. The mixture is very stiff and sticky, so this is not easy to do. If you're in a hurry, slow down; otherwise, the egg whites will break down. Finally, fold the pudding mix into a greased baking dish and cook for 40 minutes.

Another unforgettable offering was her pound cake:

## LEMON POUND CAKE

1c (2 sticks) melted butter (or canola oil)
4 eggs
1-1/2c sugar
grated peel of 1/2 lemon
juice of 1/2 lemon
1tsp vanilla extract
1/2tsp salt
1/2tsp baking powder
1/4tsp mace
1-3/4c sifted flour

Combine melted butter and eggs in a blender and blend smooth. Then add all remaining ingredients except flour and blend again. Transfer to mixing bowl, sift in 1-3/4 cups flour and mix well. Spoon into a well-greased and floured loaf or bundt pan. Bake at 325F for 55-60 minutes.

## *The Family Bond*

Grandma Finley was a unique individual and a meticulous person. Maybe that's why her date pudding always tasted so good. She readily spoke her mind, but always with love. Whenever we came in from hunting or fishing, we couldn't come inside the house until our boots were off so no dirt would be tracked into the house.

She taught us self-confidence and self-respect, to always dress nicely, be neat and stand up straight. No slouching. We usually got clothes for Christmas: a new pair of Levi's, a Pendleton shirt, a colorful sweater or a new winter jacket. I always looked forward to Christmas for the clothes. We didn't have a lot of money growing up. The special occasions were the times when we received what we really needed, and they were always nice—no discount center specials!

*Lula Mae Finley*
*my paternal grandmother*
*b. May 14, 1901 d. Feb. 13, 1983*

*Make a joyful noise unto the Lord, all ye lands. Serve the Lord with gladness: come before His presence with singing. Know ye that the Lord He is God: it is He that hath made us, and not we ourselves; we are His people, and the sheep of His pasture. Enter into His gates with thanksgiving, and into His courts with praise: be thankful unto Him, and bless His name. For the Lord is good; His mercy is everlasting; and His truth endureth to all generations.*
*Psalm 99 (100)*

I'm sure my grandmother's life perspective was shaped by her upbringing in Bonham and Dallas, Texas. Dallas had (and still has) a lot of class. The big city. She loved her family, and that in itself taught me so much. I can't think of any family members on either side of the family who didn't get along. In fact, the love and the family bond were always very strong.

Even my two brothers and I love each other and have supported each other through thick and thin all our lives. We've had our moments and our challenges, but always worked them out, because hers was the only example we ever had. Mamaw[10] made sure everybody got along. She was often quoted as saying, "You can never find happiness at the expense of someone else's happiness." Perhaps this is why she so loved the 100th Psalm.

I don't know what it was like for her, but I'm sure it must have been overwhelming when she received the news in June 1944 that her only son had been seriously wounded in the D-Day invasion of Europe at Omaha Beach in Normandy, France.[11]

The first letter she received from Daddy was not in his handwriting, and she wondered if he had been blinded by the land mine he stepped on. Fortunately, he wasn't blinded, but he didn't have use of his right hand at that time due to shrapnel wounds. Faith, hope and love sustained her. And the prayers of a mother sustained her son, my dad.

---

[10] Our nickname for Grandma Finley.
[11] Owen Jefferson Finley, Jr. was a 2nd Lieutenant in the 20th Engineer (C) Battalion that landed on Omaha Beach in the assault echelon of the 1st Infantry Division in support of the 16th Infantry Regiment on D-Day.

Before she died, we got to have one last Christmas with Mamaw in 1981. Our gift to her was our first-born son, named for both her husband and my dad, Owen Jefferson Finley III. She rejoiced at the sight and gave her six-month old great-grandson a new outfit. And yes, we had date pudding!

## Remembering Others

Grandma Finley had a sister, Aunt Alice, whom she loved dearly. We loved her too and called her "Auntie." On occasion, we would drive down to the North Park area of Dallas during the holidays to visit with her and Uncle Tom Chandler. More often than not, though, our visits to Dallas were in the summertime. Regardless of the season, Auntie always made Ambrosia.

They never had children, but Auntie had lots of nieces and nephews. Her greatest joy in life was to remember our birthdays and collect our pictures. Not long before Auntie died, I felt I should thank her for always remembering my birthday and tell her how much she meant to me. The following letter was dated April 17, 1991:

*Owen Jefferson Finley, Jr. in his World War II Army uniform, standing at the side of his house on Seneca Street in McAlester, Oklahoma*

> *Dear Auntie,*
>
> *Thank you, once again, for the birthday card and gift. I bought a new knit shirt for playing golf. You don't realize how much it means to me for you to always remember my birthday. Remembrance is one of the greatest Christian virtues, and the gift of memory has the power to transform love into life!*
>
> *You always remember and you never forget. And when you remember all the members of your family on their birthdays, I'm sure that God blesses you with an even deeper and more abiding love and joy of life than those of us who are on the receiving end.*
>
> *God bless you for always remembering. I will always remember you as the one who remembered others.*
>
> *With love,*
> *John David*

## AMBROSIA SALAD
10oz jar maraschino cherries
20oz can crushed pineapple, drained
2-11oz cans, mandarin oranges, drained
2c white mini-marshmallows
1c shredded coconut
8oz Non-Dairy Cool Whip, thawed in refrigerator overnight
1/2c chopped pecans or walnuts (optional)

Rinse cherries thoroughly, and then slice into halves. Set aside some of the cherries for garnish. Drain crushed pineapple and mandarin oranges in a strainer for several minutes. Mix marshmallows, mandarin oranges, pineapple, coconut, cherries and walnuts in a large bowl. Fold in Cool Whip slowly and carefully. Cover and chill in the refrigerator for at least 2 hours before serving. Garnish with remaining cherries and serve.

## *Christmas Eve*

Christmas at our house is centered on the services of the Church, and the foods are an indispensable part of the celebration. I especially love the Royal Hours on Christmas Eve morning. These services are so rich in theological reflection on the Incarnation of Christ, recalling not only the journey to Bethlehem and the appearance of the Angels, the Shepherds and the Wise Men, but also the flight into Egypt and the eventual settlement of the Holy Family in Nazareth.

Christmas Eve Dinner is taken early as a light but elegant ascetical meal. We usually serve angel-hair pasta with green sauce and bread, a nice bottle of Sauvignon Blanc or Chardonnay with a few cashews and medjoul dates on the side. If time permits, we might go for some fresh lobster or crab. Ambrosia Salad also makes for a nice "lite" dessert.

## ANGEL HAIR PASTA WITH GREEN SAUCE
1lb angel hair pasta
1gal water
1.5Tbl salt
1/2c extra virgin olive oil
1/3c white wine (or 2Tbl lemon juice)
2Tbl Dijon or sweet hot mustard
3 green onions, diced

1c fresh parsley, chopped
2Tbl fresh basil, chopped
4 cloves garlic, crushed and minced
Pepper to taste

*Note: As angel hair cooks rather quickly, monitor the pot carefully and have a colander preset in the sink to avoid the risk of overcooking the pasta.*

Using a large pot, add salt to water and bring to a full, rolling boil. Add pasta and stir as it begins to soften to assure the pasta doesn't stick together. Continue to boil, stirring occasionally. To test for doneness, take a piece out and taste it (careful, it's hot!) It should be al dente, which could be described as very playable, but slightly firm to the "bite." Drain immediately and transfer to serving bowl.

### GREEN SAUCE

Combine remaining ingredients in a blender or food processor and blend on high until all ingredients are thoroughly incorporated. Reserve the sauce in a cool place until ready to serve. Finally, add to drained pasta, toss thoroughly and serve hot![12]

## BROILED LOBSTER TAILS

Select fresh, live lobster from 1-1/2 to 2 lbs. To boil your lobster, fill a large stockpot with enough water to completely cover the lobster. Salt the water with rock salt (or table salt) to taste (at least 1/4 cup per gallon of water). Allow the pot to come to a full, rolling boil. You don't have to worry too much with Pacific Spiny lobsters, but the claws on Maine lobsters should be pegged or secured with bands. Grab the lobster firmly behind the head and carefully add the lobster headfirst.

Cover pot and wait for water to return to a slow boil. After returning to a slow boil, time 10 minutes for a 1-1/2 lb lobster. Add 2 minutes for each additional 1/2 pound. Immediately after boiling, pull the lobsters out of the pot with tongs, and cool them in a cold-water bath in the sink. Allow lobsters to cool for 5-10 minutes.

To clean your lobster, twist off the head and remove the greenish-yellow tomalley (liver) and the bright orange-red roe (if it's a female) then rinse the fat and guts from the body. Placing the lobster upside-down on a cutting surface, make a lengthwise cut through the tough membrane using a sharp cleaver or kitchen shears, then cut all the way through the meat and hard shell with the cleaver making two tail halves.

---

[12] Outside of the season of the fast, top pasta with grated parmesan or asiago cheese.

Place the tail halves on a baking sheet with the lobster meat facing up. Drizzle with melted margarine[13] and sprinkle with a little paprika. You can also blend the lobster roe with margarine and a little chopped parsley and salt, and baste the lobster while broiling. Place tail halves on a rack 4-6 inches from broiler. Broil 4-6 minutes (or until they begin to brown). Be careful not to overcook the lobster. Serve in shell with melted margarine. The tomalley can be blended into some melted margarine and a touch of sherry to produce a rich dipping sauce.

## WHOLE CRAB

Select fresh live crabs—the larger the better. To boil your crab, fill a large stockpot with enough water to completely cover the crab. Salt the water with rock salt (or table salt) to taste (at least 1/4 cup per gallon of water). Allow the pot to come to a full, rolling boil, and carefully add the crab. Be careful—the crab could become agitated and attempt to pinch you.

Cover pot and wait for water to return to a slow boil. After returning to a slow boil, set the cooking time for 18-20 minutes, during which you should prepare a chilled ice bath. Fill one side of the sink with ice and water. Immediately after 20 minutes of boiling, pull the crabs out of the pot with tongs, and drop them into the ice bath. Allow crabs to chill for 10 minutes. This process separates the meat from the shell and allows for ease of picking, it also seals in the flavors by stopping the cooking immediately.

To clean your crab, remove back shell, remove the lungs on top of the body and shake or rinse lightly the fat and guts from the body. The yellow stuff is called crab butter and is considered desirable by many. Rinse with cold water. Remove crab legs and crack shells with a mallet at the joints. Serve with lots of napkins, sourdough bread and melted margarine.

[13] Of course, outside the season of the fast, we use butter! Lots of butter!

## Our Mystical Journey

In the days just before Christmas I often feel that in the midst of all the hustle and bustle the world is somehow slowing down. I hear it in the Christmas carols—a world at peace, a world filled with love, a world of hope and faith. And while our society is busy trying to marginalize Christianity's influence and expressions from public life, we continue to bear witness to the birth in time of the Sun of Righteousness.

Christmas will never disappear because the One Who is outside of time entered into our time, into our world, and changed it forever. The Virgin Mary gave birth in time to One of the Holy Trinity and the world can never return to its former darkness, because Christ the Everlasting Light has been born for our salvation, at once God and man.

I am so deeply humbled and brought to my knees as I anticipate our mystical journey to Bethlehem to offer worship to Immanuel, God with us. As the final hours of the fast increase our hunger for God, and we make our way to the Christmas services, I find myself slipping into that timeless dimension of the Kingdom.

*The Nativity of Christ*

*Let us celebrate, O ye people, the feast of the Nativity of Christ, and raising our minds on high let us go in spirit to Bethlehem; and let us look upon the great mystery in the stable cave. For Eden is opened once again, when from a pure Virgin, God comes forth, perfect in His divinity as in His manhood. Therefore, let us cry: Holy God, Thou Father without beginning: Holy and Mighty, Thou Son made flesh: Holy and Immortal, Thou Spirit the Comforter: Holy Trinity, glory to Thee. 2<sup>nd</sup> Apostichon from Vespers for the Pre-feast of the Nativity of Christ.*

When I think of my experience of New Year's Day as a kid, I think of Grandpa Finley, black-eyed peas and football games. The day typically began for me by sleeping in, then going over to our grandparents' house to watch the Rose Parade (they had a color TV) and the bowl games. The main event, of course, was the Oklahoma game. More often than not, the Sooners played in the Orange Bowl, and on a few occasions against Nebraska, for the National title.

Anyway, the meal was informal. We ate in the breakfast room. Popo[14] had a way of making everything at a meal seem like it was the best he had ever eaten: "Boy, these black-eyes sure are good, Johnny. Take some more. You know, if you eat black-eyed peas on New Year's Day, you'll have money all year long!" And again: "I think this cornbread turned out to be the best I ever made. Here's some butter. You'd better butter it up while it's hot."

## BLACK-EYED PEAS

2lb dried black-eyed peas
1 ham bone from Christmas Day (or 2 ham hocks)
2 medium onions, chopped
1 green bell pepper, chopped
dried oregano to taste
3 or 4 bay leaves
1 small can whole jalapeños, seeded and diced (optional)

Soak peas in a large pot or Dutch oven overnight in water. Be sure to add water to cover two inches above the peas. They will soak up a lot of water overnight. In the morning, dump the water and peas into a strainer. Put the ham bone into the Dutch oven, then add the peas and cover with water. Add chopped onions, peppers, oregano and bay leaves.

---

[14] Our nickname for Grandpa Finley.

Bring to a boil, then turn heat down to simmer for 2-3 hours. If necessary, add water periodically to keep the water line just above the ingredients. Peas should be tender. Remove ham bone from the pot and de-bone meat. Return meat to peas and discard bone (or give a dog a bone). Serve with coleslaw, cornbread (See index) and chess pie for dessert.

## COLESLAW

1 head cabbage, finely chopped or shredded
1/2 carrot, grated
3 green onions, finely chopped
2Tbl sugar
3Tbl apple cider vinegar
salt to taste
mayonnaise (you be the judge)

Combine cabbage, carrot and green onions in a large mixing bowl. Combine sugar and vinegar. Pour over ingredients, add salt and toss. Let it set for at least an hour. Toss it occasionally. The vinegar and salt will slightly wilt the cabbage. As a result, you will not need to add as much mayonnaise when the time comes. Add mayonnaise and toss the slaw just before serving. This should produce a light, creamy consistency.

## AUNT CHRISTINE'S[15] CHESS PIE

*This is a single recipe. You might want to make a double recipe and bake two pies.*

1-1/2c sugar
3Tbl white cornmeal (yellow will do)
1Tbl white vinegar
1tsp lemon extract[16]
1/2c butter (1 stick)
4 eggs, beaten

*These were Aunt Christine's instructions:*

Mix all ingredients except butter. Then add butter and simmer on low heat until butter melts. Pour into piecrust and bake at 300F for one hour.

---

[15] My grandfather grew up on a 365-acre farm near the little town of Marietta in Cass County, Texas. His youngest brother David remained on the farm after everyone else had grown up and moved away. We used to visit Uncle Dave and Aunt Christine during the summertime. They had a huge garden across from the main house where they grew just about every kind of vegetable under the sun. Aunt Christine was a great cook. She would usually fix a big breakfast, clean up and start right in on dinner, which was served around noontime. Supper was not a cooked meal; we simply had leftovers, and the way she cooked, there was always plenty. What I remember most was her chess pie.
[16] Or grated peel and juice of 1/2 lemon.

*These are my instructions:*

Mix sugar with cornmeal by hand. Add white vinegar, lemon extract, melted butter and mix thoroughly by hand again. A blender or even an electric beater may add too much air to the mixture, creating an air pocket during baking and causing the crust to separate from the filling. Finally fold in beaten eggs and blend thoroughly. Pour into piecrust and bake at 300F for one hour.

## *A Memorable Meal*

Not only did the three Finley boys argue over who would spend the night with our grandparents on Friday nights, we also fought over who would go over to their house for dinner after Church on Sundays. Again, Daddy established a rotational system to keep the peace. More often than not, Popo would fix a rump roast, fried chicken with bread and gravy, oven-broiled T-bone steaks[17] or chicken and dumplings. I never quite mastered his ability to prepare a rump roast, fried chicken or broiled T-bones, but the chicken and dumplings...well that is a memorable meal.

### CHICKEN AND DUMPLINGS
1 whole chicken
salt
2c Bisquick
2/3c milk
1 onion, finely chopped (optional)
10oz frozen mixed vegetables (optional)

*Note: If you don't have Bisquick, use 2 cups flour, 1Tbl baking powder, and 1/2tsp salt as a substitute. Also use an egg and 5-6Tbl milk instead of 2/3 cups of whole milk.*

Add a whole chicken to a large pot or Dutch oven. Cover with water and add some salt. Bring to a boil then turn the heat down and simmer for about an hour or until the chicken is beginning to fall apart. Remove from pot and let cool for a few minutes. Remove skin and de-bone. Cut meat into small chunks and return to the chicken stock. You may want to taste the stock at this point and add a little more salt or perhaps some soy sauce. Anyway, it needs to taste good, like a soup broth.

---

[17] He would simply place a few pats of butter on each T-bone, add a little salt and stick them under the over broiler for a few minutes on each side. The melted butter helps to quickly brown the fat on the steaks without overcooking the meat.

Occasionally, I'll add some mixed vegetables and a finely chopped onion to the stock and leave it at a slow rolling boil for about 15 minutes before adding the chicken and dumplings. The end result will be a kind of potpie consistency.

In a mixing bowl, stir Bisquick and milk until soft dough forms. Drop by spoonfuls onto boiling stew; reduce heat (I like to use a melon ball scoop to form dumplings). Cook uncovered 10 min., then cover and cook 10 min. It's important not to turn the dumplings over in the stock or to pour stock over the dumplings. This will make them "gummy." Just drop them in and leave them alone. They will turn out great! Serve with a side of turnips and greens.

### TURNIPS AND GREENS

2 whole turnips, cubed
1lb frozen turnip, mustard or collard greens (of course get them fresh if they are in season and you can find them)
1Tbl butter
1Tbl vinegar
1Tbl sugar
salt to taste

Add cubed turnips to a 3-quart saucepan and cover with water. Bring to a boil and cook until turnips are tender. Add turnip greens and simmer until greens are hot. Add butter, vinegar, sugar and salt and serve.

## *The True Strength of Character*

Grandpa Finley taught my brothers and me to hunt, fish, play golf, and in general, developed within each of us an appreciation for the great outdoors. As wintertime begins to manifest the stark contrasts of evergreens with the remnants of fall colors in the trees, harvested alfalfa fields lined with dried, withered cornstalks, and dried-up creeks and rivers waiting for the gush of late winter and early spring rains—I think of him. I really miss his smile, his dry humor, his wisdom and his ability to cheer a parched soul with the waters of love, encouragement and down-home realism.

If only one of so many stories could be told that express the character of a man's man, it would be the story of the aftermath of his two-week, all-expenses-paid vacation to Guantanamo Bay, Cuba. He had served for many years as Vice President and Loan Officer of one of McAlester's local banks. The new Bank President had awarded him a trip to Cuba, which in the 1950s before the reign of Fidel Castro was a world-renowned vacation destination.

Upon his return to the bank, my grandfather, a man in his mid-sixties and nearing retirement, found the new Bank President's son sitting at his desk. His employment had been terminated and his services were no longer needed. He was given his personal belongings, including the nameplate on his desk:

**O.J. Finley**
**Vice President**[18]

Because he had made so many friends and acquaintances over the years, and secured so many loans for needy ranchers, disenfranchised African-Americans and others, he decided to go into the insurance business with the Prudential Insurance Company. Naturally, he was a success, but his true success and legacy left to our family was found in his character. After a short period of time, our grandfather went over to the banker's house, shook his hand and expressed his desire that there be no hard feelings in the matter of his untimely departure from the bank. He left his personal accounts at that bank, and asked the President for referrals for his new adventure in the insurance business.

When asked by family and friends why he extended such grace to a man who had done him wrong, he simply said, "Sometimes, you just have to be bigger than the other fellow." This indelible mark of integrity with strength of forgiveness has profoundly affected our whole family and become a motto in our lives.

*Owen Jefferson Finley, Sr.*
*my paternal grandfather*
*b. Dec. 11, 1892 d. Oct. 7, 1977*

*I love the Lord, because he hath heard my voice and my supplications. Because he hath inclined his ear unto me, therefore will I call upon him as long as I live. The sorrows of death compassed me, and the pains of hell gat hold upon me; I found trouble and sorrow. Then called I upon the name of the Lord; O Lord, I beseech thee, deliver my soul. Gracious is the Lord, and righteous; yea, our God is merciful. The Lord preserveth the simple: I was brought low, and he helped me. Return unto thy rest, O my soul; for the Lord hath dealt bountifully with thee. For thou hast delivered my soul from death, mine eyes from tears, and my feet from falling. I will walk before the Lord in the land of the living. I believed, therefore have I spoken: I was greatly afflicted: I said in my haste, all men are liars. What shall I render unto the Lord for all his benefits toward me? I will take the cup of salvation, and call upon the name of the Lord. I will pay my vows unto the Lord in the presence of all his people. Precious in the sight of the Lord is the death of his saints. O Lord, truly I am thy servant; I am thy servant, and the son of thine handmaid; thou hast loosed my bonds. I will offer to thee the sacrifice of thanksgiving, and will call upon the name of the Lord. I will pay my vows unto the Lord now in the presence of all his people, in the courts of the Lord's house, in the midst of thee, O Jerusalem. Praise ye the Lord.*[19]

[18] The nameplate from his desk at the bank is now displayed in the home of our oldest son, Owen Jefferson Finley III.

[19] I read this Psalm 116 to my Grandfather as he lay on his deathbed in McAlester General Hospital. During the last couple of years of his life, problems with his middle ears caused him to lose his balance as he walked. At the time of his death, this Psalm of triumpht gave me a vision of hope in the Resurrection and the inspiration to look forward to that day when by God's mercy and grace, his body would be raised from the dead and restored to full strength, stability and health.

## The Great Outdoors

Just a few days after New Year's Day, on January 6, we celebrate Epiphany[19] and the Great Blessing of the Waters. I especially like to conduct the Out-of-Doors Blessing of the Waters at Lake Cachuma on the Santa Ynez River in Santa Barbara County. For me, personally, it is an opportunity to deepen the sense of communion with my grandfather and to renew within myself my love for the great outdoors and all of God's beautiful creation.

We gather on the shoreline or on a boat dock, read St. Mark's short Gospel narrative on the baptism of Christ, then ask that the water may be sanctified by the power and operation and descent of the Holy Spirit; that it be given the grace of redemption and the blessing of the Jordan River.

As the cross is plunged into the depths and we sing the feast-day hymn, I feel the depth of God's love for His creation, the renewal of all things in Christ's Baptism and remember the ultimate sacrifice of His saving Passion: the Cross, the Grave and the Third Day Resurrection.

*Icon of the Theophany (Epiphany)*[20]

*When Thou, O Lord, wast baptized in the*
*    Jordan,*
*Worship of the Trinity was made manifest,*
*For the Voice of the Father bore witness of Thee,*
*Calling Thee His beloved Son,*
*And the Spirit in the likeness of a dove*
*Confirmed the Truth of His Word.*
*O Christ our God,*
*Who hath appeared and enlightened the world,*
*Glory to Thee.*

---

[20] This feast is also called Theophany, meaning "the manifestation of God," referring specifically to the manifestation of God as the Holy Trinity in the Lord's Baptism.

# CHAPTER 4 ~ *The Lenten Journey*

The Season of Lent is not something I grew up with. It is something I have learned about and begun to observe in more recent years. The reasons we enter into the discipline of fasting during this season of preparation for Easter are many. One reason is simply obedience, the "just because" reason. Christ said in His Sermon on the Mount:

> *"Moreover, when you fast, do not be like the hypocrites, with a sad countenance. For they disfigure their faces that they may appear to men to be fasting. Assuredly, I say to you, they have their reward. But you, when you fast, anoint your head and wash your face, so that you do not appear to men to be fasting, but to your Father who is in the secret place; and your Father who sees in secret will reward you openly."* Matt. 6: 2-4

Two things stand out to me in this passage: first, Jesus did not say "If you fast..." He said, "When you fast...." Historically, serious Christians always kept a Lenten fast. Secondly, what is this open reward? It is relief and freedom from sin and the growth of virtue in our lives that comes through practicing self-denial and delayed gratification. It is not that God gives us something new, which we don't already have; when God made man He called man "good." So when we diligently keep the fast with a right spirit, the darkness is quenched and the goodness within us begins to shine "openly" to others.

We become a light that will lead others to glorify our Heavenly Father.[21] It's kind of like polishing a dirty mirror until we finally see the image coming through the glass and it begins to shine. The dirt is our sins and the mirror is the image of God in each of us.

[21] Matt. 5:16

I remember once, someone asked what I was giving up for Lent. I don't like that question. It seems to shift the focus away from the goal of fasting to the means by which we fast. I said to him, "I'm giving up sin for Lent." He looked at me with a confused look on his face and didn't say anything. I smiled.

This is why it is important to go to Confession during the Lenten Season. When we confess our sins to God, our Father Confessor who is listening acts as an elder brother in the Lord to give us good advice in overcoming our sins and to assure us that God forgives us when we truly repent.[22]

*The Prophet King David*

*Have mercy upon me, O God, according to thy great mercy: according to the multitude of thy tender mercies blot out mine iniquity  Wash me thoroughly from mine iniquity, and cleanse me from my sin. For I acknowledge mine iniquity: and my sin is ever before me.  Against thee only have I sinned, and done evil in thy sight: that thou mightest be justified in thy words, and prevail when thou art judged.  For behold, I was shapen in iniquity: and in sin did my mother conceive me. For behold, thou hast loved truth: the unclear and hidden things of thy wisdom thou hast made clear to me. Thou shalt sprinkle me with hyssop, and I shall be clean: thou shalt wash me, and I shall be whiter than snow.  Thou shalt make me to hear joy and gladness: the bones which thou hast broken shall rejoice.  Turn away thy face from my sins, and blot out all my iniquities. Create in me a clean heart, O God: and renew a right spirit within me. Cast me not away from thy presence: and take not thy Holy Spirit from me. Restore unto me the joy of thy salvation: and steady me with a guiding spirit.  Then will I teach transgressors thy ways: and the impious shall be converted unto thee. Deliver me from bloodguiltiness, O God, thou God of my salvation: and my tongue shall sing aloud of thy righteousness. O Lord, open thou my lips: and my mouth shall declare thy praise. For hadst thou desired sacrifice, I would have given it thee: thou delightest not in burnt offerings. Sacrifices to God are a contrite spirit: a contrite and humble heart, O God, thou wilt not despise. Do good, O Lord, in thy good will unto Zion: that the walls of Jerusalem may be built up. Then shalt thou be pleased with the sacrifice of righteousness, with burnt offering and whole burnt offerings: then shall they offer bullocks upon thine altar.  Psalm 50(51)*

---

[22] Some may argue that it is not necessary to confess our sins in the presence of another person. To do so, however, helps us to feel the shame and realize the seriousness of our sins. King David was not led to repentance for his sin of adultery and murder until convicted by the story of the little ewe lamb told by Nathan the Prophet. At the same time, David did not receive assurance that God had put away his sin until those words were spoken to him by Nathan. (II Samuel 12:13)

## *Preparation and Fulfillment*

The Lenten style of life is something I believe can be learned only from a spiritual mentor or guide. The rules can be read and observed from a book, but the spirit of the fast can be learned only through a personal relationship with someone more spiritually mature than oneself.

In his book Liturgy and Life, Father Alexander Schmemann speaks of fasting within a context of learning how to celebrate life by developing a rhythm of preparation and fulfillment:

> *What then is celebration? It is the appropriation by us, by the Church, of the joy given by God. On the one hand, the whole life of the Church is one endless feast; and on the other hand, it is a preparation for the only ultimate feast: the fulfillment of all things, of the world itself, in God. This is why each feast, each celebration of the Church, is built on the double pattern of preparation and fulfillment.*

> *We reach Easter not by looking at the calendar and saying, "It will come on May 3." We have to go through Lent. Before Christmas we have to go through Advent. Before each feast there is always preparation, purification, fasting. When we go to Holy Communion, which is the greatest joy a man can receive, we must fast. All this reveals and teaches us the true meaning of celebration.*

> *It is easy to "go to church," it is difficult to celebrate. For mere "going to church," mere attendance is not enough. True celebration is always a living participation. But no one can reach that participation, and the meaning, the depth, the joy of the celebration, unless he prepares himself....*

> *In the Christian sense of the word, fasting is not a mere change of diet. True fasting is always bodily and spiritual, the effort of the whole man. Why? Because this is the only way for us to become light again, open to God and to His joy. It is impossible to enter the Kingdom of God without getting rid of spiritual "fat," of all that is evil, superficial, petty and mortal in our life. This is why the rhythm of the Church's life is always that of preparation and fulfillment.[23]*

---

[23] Alexander Schmemann, *Liturgy and Life*. (New York: Department of Religious Education, Orthodox Church in America, 1974) pp. 86-87.

To become "light" again. Do you hear the play on words? To become light is to overcome the darkness, but to become light is also to overcome "heaviness." Maybe this is a reference to the heaviness I experience on the bathroom scale; however it is not only a reference to the pounds I need to shed, but also to the heaviness of my sins that I need to shed. We need to become like eagles (big wings, small body) rather than chickens (big body, small wings).

> *But those who wait on the Lord shall renew their strength; they shall mount up with wings like eagles. They shall run and not be weary; they shall walk and not faint."* Isaiah 40:31

## *On the Outside Looking In*

So, our spiritual posture at the beginning of the season of the fast is an identification with Adam and Eve weeping outside the gates of Paradise because of their sin. The following hymns, sung on the evening before Lent begins, express this attitude so beautifully:

> *The Lord my Creator took me as dust from the earth and formed me into a living creature, breathing into me the breath of life and giving me a soul. He honored me, setting me as ruler upon earth over all things visible, and making me companion of the angels. But Satan the deceiver, using the serpent as his instrument, enticed me by food; he parted me from the glory of God and gave me over to the earth and to the lowest depths of death. But, Master, in compassion, call me back again.[24]*

and the second hymn:

> *O precious Paradise, unsurpassed in beauty, tabernacle built by God, unending gladness and delight, glory of the righteous, joy of the prophets, and dwelling of the saints, with the sound of thy leaves pray to the Maker of all, may He open unto me the gates which I closed by my transgression, and may He count me worthy to partake of the Tree of Life and of the joy which was mine when I dwelt in thee before.[25]*

[24] Mother Mary and Kallistos Ware, The Lenten Triodion. (London: Faber and Faber, 1977), p. 169
[25] Ibid., p. 170

## *Regaining Control*

The Lenten Season is my opportunity to regain control of my soul and body, rather than suffer the tyranny of the appetites of the flesh. In my own thinking, I have applied this verse to the Lenten discipline of fasting: "The kingdom of heaven suffers violence, and the violent take it by force."[26] This violence is the force of the will, which is required to overthrow the tyranny of the flesh. And the flesh must be weakened, through a sustained effort, in order to restore the human person as the ruler and master over his own soul and body.

This is why we fast for 40 days. When I think of a period of 40 days and its relationship to the healing of the body, I am reminded of the doctor's words to a person with a broken arm or broken leg: "It's going to have to be in a cast for 6 weeks." This is approximately the same period of time, the time of healing, the time of renewal, a time of being quiet and being still.

When Moses climbed Mount Sinai and experienced the glory of the Lord, he fasted for 40 days.[27] As a result, he was enabled to receive from God spiritual direction for the nation of Israel. By fasting for 40 days Elijah was enabled to hear the Word of the Lord in a still small voice.[28] Even Christ Himself fasted for 40 days and defeated the temptations of the devil just prior to the inauguration of His public ministry.[29] There is something about the sustained effort of the 40-day fast, when conducted with the proper motives, which produces the kind of spiritual growth we desire.

Most nutritionists promote the Lenten style of eating without even realizing it. Countless books on nutrition encourage limiting our intake of meat and of dairy products, many of which aggravate allergies. This moves our diet more toward fish, grains, vegetables and fruits. Many types of fish and edible seafood crustaceans contain omega-3 fatty acids, the best kind of fat. By returning to the basics of vegetables, fruits and grains, our fiber intake is increased, and our exposure to chemicals found in processed foods is diminished.

One might say that this has nothing to do with spirituality, or the Lenten discipline. The only point I want to make here is that the Church would not lay out a plan for us that was anything but good for us in every way. Take, for example, the Prophet Daniel and the three holy youths, Shadrach, Meshach and Abednego. He said to the steward, "Please test your servants for ten days, and let them give us vegetables to eat and water to drink...and at then end of ten days their features appeared better and fatter in flesh than all the young men who ate the portion of the king's delicacies."[30]

And what was the payoff besides winning the bet? "As for these four young men, God gave them knowledge and skill in all literature and wisdom: and Daniel had understanding in all visions and dreams."[31]

[26] Matt. 11:12
[27] Ex. 24:18
[28] I Kings 19:8-12
[29] Matt. 4:1-11
[30] Dan. 1:12, 15
[31] Dan. 1:17

## The Food Itself

Dining out during Lent seems to be somewhat of a challenge, although in recent years, especially in California, restaurants seem to have moved more towards "health conscious" menus. Lots of places, even burger joints, have "garden" burgers made with textured vegetable protein and other grains.

When ordering a green salad, ask for rice vinegar or simply a few slices of lemon on the side. You'd be amazed how good a green salad is simply with lemon juice squeezed over it. Baked potatoes can be ordered "a la carte." Try one with a side of salsa. Believe me, most restaurants want to please their customers, and so long as the request is not outrageous, they will give you what you ask for.

Here are a few of our family favorites, simple, easy and hey, maybe even fun. Our Syrian and Lebanese Christian friends, whose families and ancestors have observed the fasts of the Church since ancient times, have given many of them to us.

### LENTIL SOUP

8c water
2c dry lentils
2 onions, chopped
3-4 cloves garlic, peeled and minced
1/2c celery, sliced
2 carrots, chopped
2c chopped fresh spinach (or a 10oz pkg of frozen spinach)
1/4c lemon juice
2Tbl fresh parsley, chopped
salt, garlic powder and coriander to taste

In a large pot or Dutch oven, add lentils, onions, garlic, celery and carrots to 8 cups of water. Cook at a slow boil for about 45 minutes or until lentils and vegetables are tender. Add spinach, lemon juice, parsley and spices. Cover and turn to low heat for 20 minutes.

### TAHINI SAUCE

1/2c water
1/2c sesame tahini paste[32]
1/2c lemon juice
1Tbl fresh parsley, chopped (optional)
1tsp garlic paste (or 3 cloves garlic minced)
salt and cumin to taste

[32] Tahini paste is made from sesame seeds and has a consistency slightly thinner than peanut butter.

Simply combine ingredients in a food processor and buzz! Makes approximately 2 cups. This sauce is really good on falafel.

## Falafel (Fried Fava Bean/Chick Pea Patties)

Get it boxed from the store and follow the instructions. Sorry, I just haven't perfected a homemade recipe for this. Try to find a box that lists fava beans as the first ingredient. I like this style better.

Another suggestion—it's good to mix the package ingredients with water the day before and let set in the refrigerator overnight. This is going to give you a more solid consistency to form the slightly flattened falafel balls.

Anyway, follow the package instructions for frying. Use all-vegetable shortening for deep-fat frying. Remove them with a slotted spoon and drain on paper towels. Meanwhile, slice pocket pita bread in half, and then stuff falafel balls into the pockets along with a little chopped lettuce and sliced cucumber. Drizzle with tahini sauce and serve.

### Imjaddrah (Lentil and Bulgur Patties)
1-1/2c red lentils
4c water
1c #2 or #3 grade bulgur
salt, coriander and white pepper to taste
2 large onions, diced
1/4c extra virgin olive oil (or canola oil)
1/2c pine nuts (optional)
chopped green onions and parsley for garnish

Sort and rinse the lentils. Put them into a 3qt saucepan with the water. Bring to a boil, uncovered, and cook until tender (at least 15 minutes). Add bulgur and spices.

In a skillet, sauté diced onions in oil until golden brown. Add 1/4c water to browned onions and mash (I use a potato masher). Pour mashed onions into the bulgur and lentil mixture. If using pine nuts, add to mixture at this time. Stir and continue cooking until bulgur and lentils are done, the water has evaporated and mixture almost turns to dough. Remove from heat and let mixture set for at least one hour before serving.

Serving suggestion: Form into small patties on a platter. Garnish with sautéed onions or chopped parsley and chopped green onions.

## Lubia bi zeit (Green Bean/Tomato Stew)
3Tbl extra virgin olive oil (or canola oil)
1 medium onion, diced
1 clove garlic, minced
15oz can diced tomatoes
1lb frozen green beans (or 2-15oz cans, drained)
1c water
a touch of cinnamon and allspice to taste

Heat oil in a 3qt saucepan. Add onion and garlic and sauté over moderately high heat until onion is lightly browned. Add tomatoes, green beans and water and bring to a boil. Reduce heat and simmer, covered, for 20-30 minutes until sauce is thick. If you are using fresh green beans, cook 10-15 minutes longer or until beans are tender, adding more water if necessary. Add cinnamon and allspice to taste. Serve over Syrian rice.

## Syrian Rice
2Tbl canola oil
2Tbl orzo (rosamarina)
2Tbl fine vermicelli, broken
1c rice
3c water[33]
1/2tsp salt
a touch of cinnamon and allspice to taste (optional)

Heat oil in a large skillet. Add orzo, vermicelli and rice. Stir constantly over medium heat until browned. Does this remind you of Rice-a-Roni? Watch carefully not to burn. Add water and salt. Stir for a minute or so. Add a touch of allspice and cinnamon if you like. Bring to a boil. Reduce heat and simmer uncovered for 15-20 minutes.

Gently stir occasionally. Make sure it's not sticking to the bottom of the pan. Add a little more water if necessary. Let stand for 5-10 minutes before serving.

---

[33] Outside of Lent I use chicken broth. During Lent I'll sometimes add some vegetable boullion cubes to the water for taste.

## MIDDLE-EASTERN GARDEN SALAD

2 heads of romaine or red leaf lettuce
5 ripe tomatoes
1 large cucumber, peeled and seeded
1/2 red onion
dried spearmint leaves[34]
2Tbl extra virgin olive oil (optional)
juice of 1 or 2 lemons
garlic salt to taste

Chop lettuce, tomatoes and cucumber. Slice red onion thin. Separate rings and sprinkle into the salad. Add dried spearmint, lemon juice and toss thoroughly. Add garlic salt to taste and serve.

## LIFT (PICKLED TURNIPS)

3-4 whole medium-size turnips
3 fresh whole beets, tops off, peeled and quartered
3 cloves garlic (per jar)
2Tbl salt
2c water
1c vinegar

Wash turnips, peel white and leave purple areas of the skins, then cut into strips or wedges. Pack a few fresh beet quarters and crushed garlic cloves into three 16-ounce jars. Pack full with cut turnips. In a 1-1/2 qt saucepan dissolve salt in water and vinegar and bring to a rolling boil. Remove from heat and immediately pour over turnips until covered by liquid. Close jars tightly and store in a cool, dark place.[35] Turnips should be ready in 2-3 weeks.

[34] The dried spearmint is a critical ingredient. You may have to search for it. Try a local health food store that sells spices from bulk containers.
[35] Refer to www.homecanning.com for proper canning procedures.

## MANHATTAN STYLE CLAM CHOWDER

4-5 cloves garlic, diced
1 medium onion, chopped
1 green bell pepper, chopped
2 carrots, thinly sliced
2 ribs celery, sliced
1 large potato, sliced and chopped into small cubes
2Tbl canola oil
2c water
3 6.5oz cans chopped clams in juice
juice of 1 lemon
1Tbl Worcestershire sauce
28oz can whole peeled tomatoes, pureed in a blender
2Tbl fresh basil
1Tbl fresh parsley, chopped
1Tbl sugar
1tsp dried oregano
1/2tsp salt
1/4tsp pepper

Sauté garlic, onion, bell pepper, carrot, celery and potato in oil in a Dutch oven. Add water, juice from clams, lemon, Worcestershire sauce, and simmer for 15 minutes. Add pureed tomatoes and spices and simmer for an additional 15 minutes. Add clams just before serving.

## VEGETABLE STEW

3c water
1 stalk celery, chopped
1 large potato, chopped
1 medium onion, chopped
3-4 cloves garlic, peeled and minced
1 shallot, minced
3 bay leaves
1/2tsp salt
1/8tsp sage or poultry seasoning
1/8tsp oregano
2-15oz cans pinto beans
1-15oz can whole kernel corn
1-15oz can tomatoes, pureed

Heat water to a slow boil in a Dutch oven. Add chopped celery, potato, onion, garlic, shallot, bay leaves, salt, sage and oregano, and slow boil for about 20 minutes. Add pinto beans, corn and pureed tomatoes. Stir, turn down heat and simmer for another 10-15 minutes.

## SUCCOTASH

2Tbl canola oil
4 cloves garlic, minced
1 medium onion, chopped
1 green bell pepper, chopped
salt and pepper to taste
Tabasco Sauce and Worcestershire Sauce to taste
2-15oz cans green baby lima beans
1-15oz can whole kernel corn
1-15oz can cream-style corn
4oz jar of diced pimientos

In a 3qt saucepan, sauté fresh vegetables in oil until soft. Add spices and sauces. Combine with lima beans, corn and diced pimientos in a large pot. Mix thoroughly, then simmer for 20 minutes.

## GARDEN VEGETABLE SOUP

1-1/3c sliced carrot
1c onion, diced
4 garlic cloves, minced
6c fat free vegetable broth
3c green cabbage, thinly sliced
1c green beans
2Tbl tomato paste
1Tbl fresh basil (or 1tsp dried basil)
1tsp dried oregano
1/2tsp salt
1c chopped zucchini

In large saucepan, sprayed with nonstick cooking spray, sauté the carrot, onion and garlic over low heat until softened, about 5 minutes. Add broth, cabbage, beans, tomato paste, basil, oregano and salt; bring to a boil. Lower heat and simmer, covered, about 15 minutes or until beans are tender. Stir in zucchini and heat 3-4 minutes. Serve hot.

## FOUR-BEAN SALAD

*This is quite easy. I like to make it myself because the store-bought kind is too sweet for me.*
16oz can cut green beans, drained
16oz can cut wax beans, drained
16oz can garbanzo beans, drained
16oz can red kidney beans, drained
1 medium red onion, thinly sliced
1 fresh lemon, juiced
1-2Tbl canola or extra virgin olive oil
garlic salt to taste

Combine ingredients in a medium mixing bowl, toss thoroughly and serve.

## TEXAS CAVIAR

1lb black-eyed peas, cooked and drained
2tsp salt
2tsp ground coarse black pepper
2tsp garlic powder
1tsp ground cumin
1c celery, diced (4-5 stalks)
1 red onion, diced (a yellow or white onion is fine)
2 fresh tomatoes, diced
1 bunch fresh cilantro, washed thoroughly and chopped
1-2 jalapeño peppers, seeded and diced (optional)
3 fresh limes, juiced
6 green onions, chopped
4oz jar diced pimientos

Soak peas overnight in a large pot or Dutch oven. Drain and cook according to package directions. In a small cup, mix spices together and set aside. In a large mixing bowl, combine all remaining vegetables. Drain cooked peas and add to other ingredients. Add spices and mix thoroughly. Refrigerate overnight. Serve with tortilla chips.

## AVOCADO/SPROUT SANDWICH

Slice an avocado, remove the large pit and remove the light green meat from the peel with a large spoon. Spread some mustard on a couple of slices of whole-grain bread, then spread 1/2 ripe avocado on one bread slice. Add tomato slices, grated carrot, diced green chilies and alfalfa sprouts. For mayonnaise lovers there is a "soyonnaise" substitute that's pretty good.

## BAGEL SANDWICH

Slice and toast a bagel. I like to use an "Everything" bagel. Add mustard, thinly sliced red onions, sliced tomatoes and alfalfa sprouts. Sprinkle liberally with lemon pepper.

## *Lenten Breakfast Ideas*
Bagels with "Tofutti" (a soy-based substitute for cream cheese), or
Toast with margarine, jelly and
Fresh Fruit like an orange or apple.

**BANANA AND PEANUT BUTTER** — A MEAL IN ITSELF.

What about...

## OATMEAL
2/3c oatmeal
1-1/2c water
1/4c raisins
1Tbl maple syrup or honey
1/4tsp salt
1/8tsp cinnamon
a dash of nutmeg
1Tbl margarine

*I also like to sprinkle some Post Grape Nuts cereal or chopped walnuts on top for a little crunch.*

Place oatmeal in a 1-1/2qt saucepan and add water, raisins, maple syrup, salt and spices and bring to a boil. Stir until consistency becomes thick and begins to bubble. Cover with a lid, remove from heat and let sit for 5 minutes. Transfer to a serving bowl, add margarine and sprinkle with grape nuts. Serves one because I can't get anybody else to eat oatmeal with me in the mornings!

## HASH BROWNS WITH ONIONS
2 large (or 3 medium) potatoes
1 medium onion, diced
3Tbl canola oil
salt and pepper to taste
cayenne pepper (for the brave)

The evening before, boil potatoes for 10 minutes in a 2qt saucepan. Remove, rinse and refrigerate overnight. The next morning, peel and grate potatoes. The peel should come off by hand. Heat oil in a large cast iron skillet over medium-high heat. First add onion, then the grated potatoes. Let the potatoes begin to stick and brown, add a little salt, then take a spatula, scrape and turn potatoes. Repeat this process several times until onions and potatoes are brown and tender.

Serve with pepper and ketchup. For variety, try a little BBQ sauce or hot sauce. I also like to invent the sauce of the day. It's usually a combination of two or more of the following ingredients: ketchup, BBQ sauce, Tabasco, Tapatio Picante Sauce and salsa.

## Lenten Dessert

More often than not, my birthday falls in the season of Lent. When it does, I like to make this chocolate cake. When it doesn't, my favorite is Carrot Cake. See Index.

### CHOCOLATE CAKE

3c flour
2tsp soda
6Tbl cocoa
1tsp salt
2c sugar
3Tbl vinegar
2tsp vanilla extract
3/4c canola oil
2c cold water (or soy milk)

Measure flour, soda, cocoa, salt and sugar into large mixing bowl. Add vinegar, vanilla, oil and water and mix well. Pour batter into greased 9x13 baking pan. Bake at 350F for 45 minutes.

### FROSTING

3 sticks of margarine, softened (12oz)
1lb box powdered sugar

Blend ingredients with a mixer. If necessary, add a little warm water and blend to form a smooth, creamy texture. Frost cake after it has cooled thoroughly.

## CHAPTER 5 ~ *It is the Day of Resurrection*

Easter, or as we call it, Great and Holy Pascha, is the highest holy day of the year. Pascha, of course, is the more ancient and biblical term for Easter. It comes from the same root word as "Passover." Christ is the Paschal Lamb,[36] the ultimate Passover sacrifice.

Our annual observance of Holy Week leads up to Easter Sunday, followed by a week of festive services and food called "Bright Week." On Great and Holy Friday of Holy Week we have no food. On Great and Holy Saturday we fix food. And on the Great and Holy Pascha we eat food, both heavenly and earthly!

## *Three Great Condescensions*

In Christ we bear witness to three great condescensions (or descents): The first comes in the Incarnation itself, the Nativity of our Lord; the second in His descent into the waters of Baptism; and the third in His Crucifixion and descent into Hell.

These three great descents are reflected in our Church art. In the Icon of the Nativity we see Jesus wrapped in swaddling clothes, yet a closer look reveals them as burial wrappings. The Lord came into this world to die and so from the very beginning of our celebration of God become man, we are reminded that our Lord came to save us through His death on the Cross.

*"And being found in appearance as a man, He humbled Himself and*
*became obedient to the point of death, even the death on the Cross."*
Phillipians 2:8

In the icon of the Lord's Baptism, we celebrate the sanctification and renewal of the fallen creation in the descent of the Lord of Glory into the waters of the Jordan River.

---

[36] St. Paul says, "...For indeed Christ, Our Passover, was sacrificed for us." I Cor. 5:7.

In His third and final descent the Lord, strong and mighty, the Lord mighty in battle, the Lord of Hosts, the King of Glory descends[37] into the dust of death.[38]

Many sincere people are either totally unaware of Christ's Descent into Hell to which the Apostle's Creed[39] refers, or perhaps suspicious that this is not a biblical teaching. Nothing could be further from the truth. In St. Peter's famous sermon found in the second Chapter of Acts, he applies Psalm 15(16):8-11 prophetically to Christ's descent into Hell stating that in Hades, the Lord Jesus "loosed the pains of death, because it was not possible that He should be held by it."[40]

In his first General Epistle, St. Peter again refers to the Lord's descent to those in darkness and death saying the Lord "went and preached to the spirits in prison."[41] and again "...the Gospel was preached to those who are dead...."[42]

Surely, the Lord's Mother felt a kind of pain experienced by no other mother in the history of the human race. She, whose body experienced no pain in the miraculous birth of her only Son and our God, is now pierced in her own soul[43] with the sword of Jesus' immeasurable suffering and death on the Cross.

But from the depths of our sorrow, through the hymns of the Church, we hear with our spiritual ears and see with our spiritual eyes what we are otherwise unable to behold and comprehend: the words of Jesus comforting his mother and announcing to all creation His Resurrection from the dead:

> *"Mourn not for me, Mother, as thou beholdest me in the grave: for I thy Son, whom thou didst conceive in thy womb without seed, shall rise and shall be glorified...."*[44]

---

[37] *From the Heights Thou didst descend, O Compassionate One.*
*And Thou didst submit to the three-day burial*
*That Thou might deliver us from passion,*
*Thou are our Life, and our Resurrection, O Lord, glory to Thee.*
*(Tone 8 Resurrection Troparion)*
[38] My strength is dried up like a potsherd, and my tongue clings to my jaws; you have brought me to the dust of death. Psalm 21(22):15
[39] I believe in God the Father Almighty, Maker of heaven and earth. And in Jesus Christ his only Son our Lord; who was conceived by the Holy Ghost, born of the Virgin Mary, suffered under Pontius Pilate, was crucified, dead, and buried; he descended into hell; the third day he rose again from the dead; he ascended into heaven, and sitteth on the right hand of God the Father Almighty; from thence he shall come to judge the quick and the dead. I believe in the Holy Ghost; the holy Catholic Church; the communion of saints; the forgiveness of sins; the resurrection of the body; and the life everlasting. Amen.
[40] Acts 2:24
[41] I Peter 3:19
[42] I Peter 4:6
[43] Luke 2:35
[44] From the 9th Ode of the Canon for Great and Holy Saturday Matins.

## The Harrowing of Hell

This great and final descent in Hell, the extreme humility of our Savior, is so beautifully expressed in the Church's hymnody of Great and Holy Saturday. In these hymns we see over and over again this image of the Lord, descending into depths, to the bottoms of the mountains, into the pit of the earth with its chains and bars[45], the darkest place of corruption, in search of a man, a special man, the first man the Lord ever made—Adam—and with him, our first mother, Eve.

*Christ raising up Adam and Eve and releasing them from Hell*

When Satan tempted the Lord on the Mountain, he was busy trying to figure out whether Jesus was the Son of God. But he couldn't figure it out. How does one understand the Mystery of God become Man? When our Lord Jesus Christ descended into hell as a man, Satan thought he had conquered Him, because all he saw was a man. He accepted Him into his domain, the Kingdom of death, but the Lord's Divinity was hidden in His humanity like a fishhook inside a fish. When the Devil took the bait, Christ set the hook and in one fell swoop, darkness was filled with light and death was filled with life!

While in the grave with His body and at the same time in paradise with the repentant thief and on the throne with the Father and the Spirit, Jesus was in Hell with His soul as God, trampling down Death by His death.

> *"The company of the angels was amazed when they beheld Thee numbered among the dead. Yet Thou, O Savior destroyed the power of death and with Thyself raising up Adam and releasing all men from Hell."[46]*

> *"The Pure Temple hath been destroyed, then rising; he raised with him the fallen tabernacle; for the second Adam who dwelleth in the highest, hath descended unto the first Adam in the uttermost chambers of hades...."[47]*

---

[45] Psalm 106(107):14-20
[46] First Troparion of the Blessed Hymns of Great and Holy Saturday.
[47] Eighth Ode, First Troparion, Matins of Great and Holy Saturday.

Quoting the Psalmist, St. Paul refers to Christ's defeat of Hell:

*"When He ascended on high, He led captivity captive and gave gifts to men."* Psalm 67(68):18

*"(Now this, 'He ascended' – what does it mean but that He also first descended into the lower parts of the earth? He Who descended is also the One who ascended far above all the heavens, that He might fill all things.)* Ephesians 4:8-10

## *Baptized into Christ*

Pascha is first and foremost a baptismal feast. The Epistle Lesson for Great and Holy Saturday is taken from St. Paul's Letter to the Romans:

*Or do you not know that as many of us as were baptized into Christ were baptized into His death...for if we have been united together in the likeness of His death, certainly we also shall be in the likeness of His resurrection.* Romans 6:3-5

We read the account of the Creation of the Universe on this day. The first created matter mentioned in the Genesis account is water. Does it not seem fitting then, that the Lord would use water to renew the fallen man and to raise him to eternal life?

The waters of baptism contain the power of the waters of the Red Sea, and just as Moses stretched out his hand in the sign of the Cross over the waters, so too, the priest makes the sign of the Cross over the baptismal waters.[48]

In the Red Sea the enemies of God's chosen people were crushed beneath the waters, unable to pass through to the other side. In the same way, we pray that the enemies of redeemed Israel—that is, the devil and his demons—be destroyed by the holy baptismal waters, and that these hostile powers flee from it, unable to conceal themselves or to descend into this fountain of incorruption.

---

[48] Ex. 14:21-19. Inscribing the invincible weapon of the Cross upon the waters, Moses marked a straight line before him with his staff and divided the Red Sea, opening a path for Israel who went over dry-shod. Then he marked a second line across the waters and united them in one, overwhelming the chariots of Pharaoh. Therefore let us sing to Christ our God, for He has been glorified. (Irmos of Canticle One for the Feast of the Exaltation of the Cross on September 14)

And just as the Children of Israel came up out of the water singing the Song of Victory, the Song of Moses,[49] so too, we sing our victorious song when the newly baptized emerge from the waters of regeneration: "As many of you as have been baptized into Christ have put on Christ. Alleluia."[50]

Christ said, "For as Jonah was three days and three nights in the belly of the whale, so will the Son of Man be three days and three nights in the heart of the earth."[51] Jonah was saved through water in the belly of that great fish, having first been swallowed, then returned to dry land at the command of the Lord. So too, are we saved through water in the baptismal font, the womb of the Church, our Mother,[52] and are brought forth as adopted children of the heavenly Father.[53]

Finally, when we hear the familiar story of the Three Holy Children in the fiery furnace read at this great and glorious baptismal feast, our hearts burn with zeal for the house of God rejoicing in the power of the new birth.

We are all familiar with the story of Moses and the Burning Bush. The uncreated fire of God engulfed the bush, yet did not consume it. In a similar way, God protected Shadrach, Meshach and Abednego in the fiery furnace appearing in the flames with them and making the flames like dew.

This foreshadowing of the Incarnation and of Baptism is revealed in some small way through the ancient Christian illustration of the sword in the fire:

*The Three Holy Children in the Fiery Furnace*

> *Imagine a steel sword being heated in a fire. The sword becomes red hot... The sword is still distinctly steel and the fire is still distinctly fire. The steel does not become fire, nor does the fire become steel. But the sword does get hot. It partakes of the heat of the fire. The heat of fire, the energy of the fire, interpenetrates the substance of the sword...*

> *As the energy of the fire interpenetrates the sword and in so doing heats it, so the divine nature of Christ interpenetrates His human nature with the divine energies—such as wisdom, love, and holiness.[54]*

---

[49] Exodus 15:1-18
[50] Galatians 3:27
[51] Matthew 12:40
[52] "...but the Jerusalem above is free, which is the mother of us all." Galatians 4:26
[53] Thou didst descend to the nether regions of the earth, O Christ, and shattered the eternal bars that held us prisoners captive, and as Jonah from the whale, thou hast risen as almighty. (6th Irmos of the Paschal Canon)
[54] Jon Braun, *Divine Energy*, Ben Lomond, CA.: Conciliar Press, 1991, pp.74-75

When we are baptized into Christ, we are substantially united to His Life-giving Flesh which is forever, interpenetrated by the uncreated energies from His Divine Nature. The baptismal font becomes a fiery furnace as well as a water grave and we die with him, we are buried with Him, and we are raised with Him, on fire for God, clothed with the dignity of immortality[55] and shining like the stars of heaven.[56]

After the Apostle Philip had opened the meaning of the scriptures to the Ethiopian Eunuch, they came to some water.

> *And the Eunuch said, "See here is water. What hinders me from being baptized?" Then Philip said, "If you believe with all your heart, you may." And he answered and said, "I believe that Jesus Christ is the Son of God." So he commanded the chariot to stand still. And both Philip and the eunuch went down into the water, and he baptized him.* Acts: 8: 36-38

Do you believe with all your heart? I do.

On this great and holy day all who have been baptized into Christ find in this celebration the remembrance of their own baptism transformed into reality. And for those who have not been baptized into Christ, the invitation is extended, "Ho, everyone who thirsts, come to the waters!"[57]

## *Early in the Morning Let Us Arise*

Before the dawn, before the first light of Pascha morning, we gather into the Church once again with great anticipation of the Resurrection revealed. The Church becomes a manifestation of the dark tomb in which the precious Body of Christ had lain. But from this darkness comes a glimmer of light, a glimmer of hope and a glimmer of triumph as the priest emerges from the Altar with the Paschal Candle singing:

> *Come ye, take Light from the Light that is never overtaken by night.*
> *Come glorify the Christ, risen from the dead.*

---

[55] He Who delivered the children from the furnace, and became man, and suffered as a mortal, and through His suffering, clothes the mortal with the dignity of immortality, He is the only blessed God of our Fathers. (7th Irmos of the Paschal Canon)
[56] Matthew 13:43
[57] Isaiah 55:1

And as we receive the light with our baptismal candles we make our way in procession around the cold and dark Church singing:

*Thy Resurrection, O Christ our Savior, the angels in heaven sing.*
*Enable us on earth, to glorify Thee in purity of heart.*

Then we gather at the doors of the Church and hear St. Mark's Gospel account of the Resurrection and respond with indescribable joy singing the glorious Paschal Hymn:

*Christ is risen from the dead, trampling down death by death, and*
*upon those in the tombs bestowing life.*

The Priest as the living icon of Christ in our midst turns and bangs on the doors as if banging down the gates of hell, shouting:

*Lift up your heads, O ye gates; and be ye lifted up, ye everlasting*
*doors: and the King of glory shall come in.*

*"Who is the King of Glory?"* cries the feeble voice of the devil from behind the doors.

*The Lord strong and mighty, the Lord mighty in battle. The Lord of*
*hosts, He is the King of Glory!*

Our eyes are flooded with the light from the empty tomb as we enter the Church rejoicing in song.[58]

## *The Meaning of Pascha*

The Great and Holy Pascha is not merely a time to remember what Christ did for us in His Saving Passion, but to transform this remembrance into the reality of our lives. We not only remember our baptism, we also put on Christ in a new way. "...Likewise you also, reckon yourselves to be dead indeed to sin, but alive to God in Christ Jesus our Lord."[59]

The Great and Holy Pascha may be the end of our Lenten Journey, but it is also the beginning of the Christian Life. "Now if we died with Christ, we believe that we shall also live with Him."[60] Therefore, may our light shine in the darkness and may the darkness not over-

---

[58] If you never have before, visit an English-speaking Orthodox Christian Church for the midnight Easter Service.
    Years ago Christianity Today Magazine called it a "Spiritual Super Bowl!"
[69] Romans 6:11
[60] Rom. 6:8

come it. And in everything we think, say or do, may we bear witness to the true Light, our Lord and God and Savior Jesus Christ, Who is risen from the dead.

St. John the Evangelist says in the Gospel Lesson for Pascha, "As many as have received Him, to them our Lord has given power to become children of God...and of His fullness we have all received, and grace for grace."[61]

## *Breaking the Fast*

In the Book of Genesis we find that Abraham offered, instead of his son, a ram provided by God.[62] We also read in the same book where Abel offered the firstborn of his flock, and the Lord respected Abel and his offering.[63] In both cases, the lamb is understood as a type of the Passover sacrifice, which is a type of Christ.

In the Gospel of Luke we read where the father killed the fatted calf for his prodigal son who had returned. This was an act of restoration to communion with his father and cause for a great festival.[64] In the following prayer, said as we break the fast from flesh-meats, we see these foreshadowings of Christ fulfilled in the Paschal Celebration:

> *Look down, O Lord Jesus Christ our God, upon these flesh-meats,*
> *and sanctify them, as Thou didst sanctify the ram which faithful*
> *Abraham offered unto Thee, and the lamb which Abel brought unto*
> *Thee as a whole burnt-offering; also the fatted calf which Thou didst*
> *command to be slain for Thy son who had gone astray and had*
> *returned again to Thee, that, even as he was accounted worthy to*
> *enjoy Thy grace, so may we also enjoy these things which are sancti-*
> *fied and blessed by Thee, to the nourishment of us all. For Thou art*
> *our true Nourishment and the Giver of all good things, and unto*
> *Thee we ascribe glory, together with Thine unoriginate Father and*
> *Thine all holy and good and life-giving Spirit, now and ever and*
> *unto ages of ages. Amen.*

In the Book of Exodus we see the Promised Land described as "a land flowing with milk and honey." In his invitation to the abundant life, the Prophet Isaiah describes the kingdom of God as a place to "come, buy wine and milk without money and without price."[65] And again the prophet Joel says, "And it will come to pass that the mountains shall drip with new wine, the hills shall flow with milk...."[66]

[61] John 1:12,16
[62] Genesis 22:13
[63] Genesis 4:4
[64] Luke 15:23
[65] Isaiah 55:1
[66] Joel 3:18-21

Having completed our abstention from all animal by-products (dairy products) we continue our Paschal celebration of the Kingdom of God and the Promised Land restored through this Prayer for Cheese and Eggs:

*O Master, Lord our God, the Creator and Maker of all things: Bless Thou this cheese and likewise these eggs, and preserve us in Thy goodness. That as we partake of them, even so also, we may be filled with Thy gifts, which ungrudgingly Thou bestowest, and with Thine unspeakable goodness. For Thine is the might and the kingdom and the power and the glory of the Father and of the Son and of the Holy Spirit, now and ever and unto ages of ages. Amen.*

## Food Glorious Food

### HAM

Ham[67] pretty much says it all for me at Pascha. Living in Tennessee after college, I got hooked on country ham and red-eye gravy. It's almost impossible to find country ham in California, so I just slice up regular old sugar-cured ham and simmer it in coffee for a few minutes. It goes great on a biscuit, a bagel, or just by itself with a side of scrambled eggs.

### HARD-BOILED EGGS

Hard-boiled eggs are pretty basic-you need a pan, some eggs, water and some heat. I usually boil them for about 10 minutes. Don't start the timer, though, until the water is boiling. It doesn't have to be a rolling boil, but on the other hand, they don't call 'em "hard-boiled" eggs for nothin'. After 10 minutes of boiling, I immediately take them off the heat, pour out the hot water and add ice-cold water to cool them off and stop the cooking process. They can then be peeled and eaten.

The peeling process can be a pain. Here's what I do, but I'm never 100% successful: Crack the hard shell over the entire surface of the egg. As you begin to peel off the shell, try to get under the membrane located between the egg and the shell. If you can do this, the shell will sometimes come off practically in one piece. Otherwise you can pick away at it for what seems to be an eternity and your egg will end up looking like it has "chicken pox." Fresh eggs peel 10

---

[67] I prefer the butt end over the shank end of a half ham. It's fairly easy to de-bone into three sections, leaving the bone for soup or a pot of beans in about a week. You can actually see these sections (muscles) separated by thin layers of fat. I just pierce through the meat with a filet knife along that line to the other side and carve each section from the bone. The fat is then easy to trim and I end up with three nice lean boneless sections ready to slice.

times better than your basic supermarket 3-week-old eggs. Try to find some fresh brown cage-free or organic eggs. You won't be sorry you spent a little extra money when you discover how easily they peel.

## RED-DYED EGGS[68]

12 fresh eggs
1fl oz red food dye
2-1/2c hot water
1/2c vinegar

Place eggs in a 3qt saucepan, cover with water and bring to a boil. Reduce heat and simmer for 15 minutes. Meanwhile, dissolve dye in hot water and vinegar. After the eggs are cooked, transfer them to the dye mixture. Leave them in the dye for about 10 minutes or until the eggs reach the desired color. Dry eggs on a wire rack. After drying, shine them up with a lightly-oiled cloth.

## DEVILED EGGS

I've never followed a precise recipe for deviled eggs, but I can describe what I do: Slice peeled hard-boiled eggs with a sharp knife. Carefully remove yolks and place in a small mixing bowl. Salt and pepper the yolks, squirt them with some prepared mustard, quite a few shakes of Tabasco or Tapatio Picante Sauce, then mash them with a fork. Blend in enough mayonnaise to create a smooth, creamy consistency. Carefully spoon into the hollowed out portions of the solid egg whites, and sprinkle with paprika for decoration.

## PASCHA CHEESE

There's this wonderful spread called "Pascha Cheese." It's a Russian thing, almost like cheesecake, and it's awesome. It will also make you fat if you eat too much of it. It is traditionally served on special bread called Kulich *(See following recipe).*

---

[68] Red-dyed eggs proclaim our redemption by the blood of the Risen Lord. After the priest blesses the eggs and before we eat them, we tap them against each other, saying, "Christ is Risen! He is Risen, indeed!" Cracking the egg reveals the breaking of the seal of Christ's tomb and the rolling away of the stone. The egg itself manifests our new life in Christ.

After our Lord's Ascension into Heaven, St. Mary Magdalene, an eyewitness of the Resurrection, traveled to Rome and appeared before Tiberius Caesar. She presented him with a red-colored egg and greeted him with the words: "Christ is Risen!" At the same time, she accused Pilate before Caesar for his unjust condemnation of the Lord Jesus. Caesar accepted her accusation and transferred Pilate from Jerusalem to Gaul where, in disfavor with the emperor, he later died. In her icon, St. Mary Magdalene is often depicted holding a red-colored egg in her hand.

3/4lb (3 sticks) unsalted butter, softened
3lb cheese (made from 2 gal buttermilk) or you can use farmer's cheese
3c sugar
9 egg yolks
2 vanilla beans (or 1T extract)
1-1/2tsp salt
24oz whipping cream (or sour cream)
1-1/2c golden raisins (optional)
1c blanched almonds, finely chopped (optional)

Set out butter to soften at room temperature. Pour 2 gal buttermilk into deep baking dishes and place in a low oven (200 to 250F) until the curds separate from the whey (1 to 1-1/2 hr). Strain curds in three layers of cheesecloth in a colander till dry. Placing a plate with a heavy object on the top of the cheese can accelerate this process. Let cheese sit for at least two hours. Put cheese in a large mixing bowl and set aside.

Blend softened butter, sugar, egg yolks, the insides of the vanilla beans and salt with an electric mixer on high speed. Add mixture to bowl of strained cheese and thoroughly mix by hand with a wooden spoon. Whip cream with electric mixer until stiff. Add whipped cream (or sour cream), raisins and chopped almonds. Chop one of the beans until fine and add to mixture or use vanilla extract if beans are unavailable. Mix quickly and thoroughly.

Line two 7-1/2" clay flowerpots with cheesecloth. Pour mixture into flowerpots and cover with cheesecloth. Set pots on a wire rack placed on a cookie sheet. Refrigerate for at least 24 hours. Up to a week is best.

Unmold and decorate as desired. Slice with a cake server. Serve cold on Kulich bread. Take a bite, then say, "Christ is Risen! He is Risen, indeed!"

## KULICH
3 packages dry yeast
1/4c warm water
1-1/2c milk
3/4c butter
1-1/2c flour
1Tsp vanilla extract (or 1 vanilla bean, finely chopped)
9 eggs, separated
2c sugar

1/2tsp cardamom
1/2tsp nutmeg
3-1/2c flour or more as needed (dough should be slightly sticky)
3Tbl rum
1/2c each: candied fruit, blanched slivered almonds, golden raisins (all optional)

In a small bowl, sprinkle the yeast over 1/4c of warm water (105-109F) and make a paste. Let it sit about 7 minutes. Add about 2tsp flour and 1/8tsp sugar. Set in a warm place to rise (about 30 min.).

Bring the milk to a boil, then add the butter so it melts in the milk. Place the flour in a bowl, pour the hot milk and butter over it, and mix until smooth. Set aside.

Beat two of the egg whites until stiff, and set aside. Cream the 9 yolks with two cups sugar, and set aside.

After the mixture of milk, butter and flour has cooled considerably, add the egg yolk, sugar mixture and yeast. Combine thoroughly, then fold in egg whites and spices.

Slowly mix in 3-1/2c flour. Lastly add 3Tbl rum. Add additional flour as needed to make the dough (which should be slightly sticky and at the point where it just falls off your fingers.) If using candied fruit, add at this time.

Place the dough in ungreased, foil-lined oatmeal canisters or coffee cans to a height of half the desired height of the baked kulich. This recipe will make 3 small (or 1 large and 1 small) kulichi. Allow to rise for 40 minutes to an hour, then bake for 1 hour at 350F (larger kulichi will have to bake longer). Allow to cool for 15 min. in forms, then turn out onto wire rack to cool completely.


## Easter Baskets

My wife Janni always goes out of her way to prepare Easter baskets for the family. The main thing is chocolate candy: chocolate malt balls, Reese's Miniature Peanut Butter Cups, Snickers, Peanut M&M's, jellybeans, the works! She also includes one or two gifts.

I have to go for the milk when we dive into the baskets. A tall glass of milk complements the chocolate candy so well, but seems to produce a vicious cycle of more candy, more milk, more candy, and more milk... It's amazing how much weight a person can gain back in a week if he is not careful.

## Country Breakfast

### BISCUITS

2-1/4c Original Bisquick
2/3c milk
all-purpose white flour

Heat oven to 450F. In a medium mixing bowl, stir ingredients until soft dough forms. Turn onto surface sprinkled with all-purpose white flour. Knead dough, adding flour until it is no longer sticky. Roll out or flatten dough to about 1/2" thick. Cut with 2-1/2" cutter (or use a drinking glass). Place on a baking sheet and bake 8-10 minutes. Makes 9 biscuits.

### SAUSAGE

1lb hot country-style pork sausage

Preheat cast iron skillet on medium high. Place patties in skillet and cook on each side for 5 minutes or until done. To test for doneness, press on patties with a spatula. When no blood is visible and liquid is clear the patties are done. Drain on a platter with a paper towel.

### SAUSAGE GRAVY

2Tbl flour
1-1/2-2c hot milk
2Tbl chopped parsley
2 sausage patties, diced
salt to taste

From the same skillet used to fry sausage, drain off all grease except 2Tbl Stir in flour and cook thoroughly to form a roux.[69] Slowly add hot milk and stir constantly pressing out all lumps to form a smooth gravy. Add diced sausage. Add a little salt to taste. Serve over warm opened biscuits and garnish with parsley and lots of black pepper.

---

[69] A "roux" is a mixture of flour and fat cooked together and used as a thickening.

## SCRAMBLED EGGS

2 eggs per person
1Tbl water per egg
salt to taste

Heat frying pan on medium. Add 1tsp butter or margarine per egg to be scrambled. (Hint: Most sticks of butter or margarine are marked by tablespoon. 3tsp=1Tbl. In a medium mixing bowl beat eggs, water and salt thoroughly. Add to frying pan and stir with a spatula constantly until eggs are done to your liking.

## GRITS

4c water
1tsp salt
1c grits

Bring water and salt to a boil in a 2qt saucepan; slowly stir in grits. Cover pan; reduce heat to low. Cook, stirring occasionally, for 5 to 6 minutes. Yields 4 cups. Serve with butter or milk and sugar.

## CHEESE GRITS CASSEROLE

3c water
1tsp salt
3/4c quick grits
2c shredded cheddar cheese (8oz net weight)
3/4c milk
1/3c butter or margarine, softened
2 large eggs, lightly beaten
6-12 drops hot pepper sauce
1/4tsp ground black pepper

Preheat oven to 375F. Grease a 2-qt baking dish. Bring water and salt to a boil in a 3qt saucepan; slowly stir in grits. Cover pan; reduce heat to low. Cook, stirring occasionally, for 5 to 6 minutes. Add 1-1 /2 cups cheese, milk and butter to saucepan; stir until cheese and butter are melted. Add eggs, hot pepper sauce and pepper; stir well. Pour into prepared baking dish; sprinkle with remaining cheese. Bake for 40-45 minutes or until golden brown and puffy. Let stand for 5 minutes before serving.

## CODDLED EGGS

It's always fun to come back to eggs on cheese toast for breakfast during the Easter Season. This is something I learned from a Vietnam Vet who lived with me for a few months back in 1978. It's a coddled egg. Growing up in Oklahoma I never heard of a coddled egg; I had heard of a poached egg and didn't like it, but never a coddled egg. Somehow, with the years our tastes change.

Bring some water to a boil in a 1-1/2qt saucepan, then stir it around and around creating a funnel in the pan. Quickly crack open one or two eggs and drop them into the swirling water. Turn down the heat and simmer covered for about three minutes.

Carefully remove the egg(s) from the pan with a slotted spoon and place them on a nice hot piece of cheese toast. The "middle" (that's what we call it in Oklahoma) should be runny if cooked properly. Mmmm good! Tabasco or Tapatio Picante Sauce on top really hits the spot if you like it hot.

## BACON

Place separated slices in an unheated frying pan. Cook slowly for 6-8 minutes over moderately low heat, turning slices occasionally. When bacon is crisp, remove from pan and drain on paper towels.

### LIT'L SMOKIES (WRAPPED IN CRESCENT DINNER ROLLS)
1 canister Crescent Dinner Rolls
1lb Lit'l Smokies

Remove crescent dinner roll dough from packaging. There are usually 8 triangle rolls in a canister. With a knife, cut each roll in half lengthwise creating 16 thin triangle rolls. Place a Lit'l Smokie at the thick end and roll each one up in a cylindrical ball. Place on a baking sheet and bake at 375F for 11-13 minutes. Serve with jelly and a cup of coffee!

## CHAPTER 6 ~ *Bobby-Que*

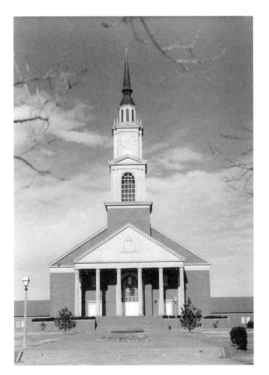

*Raley Chapel on the campus of OBU*

As a student at Oklahoma Baptist University in the early 1970s, I used to take a special trip about once a week to a little rib shack in Shawnee called the Elite Cafe. I didn't have a car, so I would hustle around campus until I could find somebody with a car who would go with me.

Juanita, owner of the Elite, made the best pork BBQ spareribs in a brick oven with an offset firebox. The meat just fell off the bone! But what even surpassed her ribs was her sauce. She had three plastic bottles at each table: green, orange and red. It didn't take this rocket scientist very long to break the code. The green bottle was mild, the red, hot, and the orange, a cautious mix. I still dream about it.

Anyway, Juanita never would give me the recipe for her secret sauce, but I looked on her shelves and tried to figure out the ingredients. In that process, I discovered a few of her secret ingredients. Over the years, I have tried to come up with a close imitation. The following recipe has never quite matched my memory of her sauce, but the dream is still there.

## Juanita's BBQ Sauce — almost

2c tomato puree
1c French dressing
1/2c brown sugar
1/4c prepared mustard
1/4c apple cider vinegar
2Tbl Worcestershire Sauce
2Tbl corn oil
1Tbl Tabasco Sauce
1tsp salt
1tsp black pepper
1tsp garlic powder

Add all ingredients to a blender and process. Makes about 1qt.

## Pork BBQ Spare Ribs

Plan for at least one pound of ribs per person. A slab can weigh anywhere from 3 to 4-1/2lbs. To prepare the slabs for the grill, remove the tough thin membrane from the backside of the ribs. I usually have to start the process with a knife until I can grab it with my hand and pull it off. This is not necessary, but makes the ribs easier to eat.

I also like to rub in a combination of spices. Any kind of seasoned pepper blend will do, but if you don't have anything on hand, use the BBQ Rub below, which should make more than enough for two slabs of ribs.

I like to use a rib rack and place them tip-side down. The indirect method on a Weber grill is the best for maximizing flavor,[70] unless of course, you have an offset firebox smoker. The ribs can be cooked flat out the conventional way, but you have to watch them closely and keep turning them.

Plan on leaving the ribs on the grill for at least two hours when using the indirect method on the Weber. The ribs should be done when the skin begins to split. Another way to test doneness is to insert a knife between the ribs and twist. If the meat begins to separate from the bone, they're done. Baste the ribs with Juanita's sauce for another 10 minutes before removing them from the grill. Enjoy with garlic bread or cornbread and coleslaw (See index).

---

[70] Note: It is not uncommon to boil ribs before placing them on the grill. This may insure tenderness, but it will also insure a significant loss in flavor, shifting the focus from the ribs to the sauce. Juanita did not boil her ribs.

## Santa Maria Style Tri-Tip BBQ

Unless one is from California, and Santa Barbara County in particular, he or she may never have heard of tri-tip. At least my first encounter with this wonderful triangular piece of meat came after moving to Southern Cal. Tri-tip is not a "cut;" rather, it is a whole muscle in the bottom beef sirloin area. Meat packers from all over the country send tri-tips to California.

The best way to purchase tri-tip is by the bag. There are usually 6 tips per bag. Each tri-tip will have a large top layer of fat, most of which needs to be trimmed. There is a very spongy membrane on top of the fat layer that definitely needs to come off. I like to continue trimming the fat down, leaving just a thin layer.

Tri-tips can go right on the Weber as is. The Tri-tip and Chicken Marinade which follows is awesome. If I don't have time to marinade overnight or at least 4 hours, I pack them with seasoning. Suzie Q's Brand Santa Maria Style Seasoning[71] is a local favorite, but anything you like will do. If I'm not in too big a hurry, I'll mix up the following, which works pretty well for tri-tips, and for ribs, chicken and steaks as well:

### BBQ Rub
2Tbl paprika
1Tbl salt
1Tbl garlic powder
1Tbl black pepper
1Tbl chili powder
1Tbl brown sugar
1/2tsp cayenne pepper (optional)

Mix thoroughly. Sprinkle meat liberally by hand on all sides. Rub in seasoning by hand. Depending on how much meat you are cooking at once, you may not use the whole mixture or you may need to make more.

The most authentic approach to tri-tip barbecue is "open-pit" with live red oak coals. The oak imparts a distinctive flavor, and once you recognize and develop a taste for it, any other way doesn't quite measure up. When using the open pit method, the meat needs to be turned often and may take up to an hour to cook—depending on the temperature of the fire, the outside temperature and the thickness of the tri-tip. In a Weber Grill, I like to cook them "lid on" for about 25 minutes, fat side up. You can turn them once, placing fat side down, but only for about five minutes, then turn them back "fat side" up.

People often comment on the tri-tip's tenderness when I serve it and ask what my secret is.

[71] SusieQ's Brand can be ordered from http://www.susieqbrand.com/. You can also find a store locater on this site.

Well, it's not the rub, the marinade, the coals or the grill—it's the way I slice it. You have to slice against the grain. If you don't look carefully, you will likely cut a tri-tip with the grain just because of its shape. You wouldn't believe how many people make this mistake. The meat becomes very tough to chew, so look before you slice and slice against the grain.

## BBQ Chicken

I like to use small chickens. When I was a kid, a 3-pound chicken was pretty standard. These days, a 3-3-1/2 pounder is actually kind of hard to find. But it works best if you can find one. Remove the back with a meat cleaver or large, hefty butcher knife and split the breast right down the middle. This will leave two halves for the BBQ. Sprinkle and rub in BBQ seasoning. Cook skin side up, rib cage and bone side down. Grill over medium heat using the indirect method. The last 15 minutes, baste with Juanita's BBQ Sauce.

*Note: If you decide to use the Tri-Tip/Chicken Marinade below, the basting won't be necessary.*

The best way to test for doneness is to pull on the leg to see if the thigh will separate from the breast. If it will, it's done.

### Tri-Tip and Chicken Marinade
1 onion, sliced in 1/4" wedges
12fl oz beer
1c soy sauce
1-1/2c water
1Tbl crushed garlic
juice of 2 lemons, or 4 limes[72]
coarse ground black pepper to taste (use a lot)
Suzie Q's Santa Maria Style Seasoning (or California Style Garlic Salt) to taste

Rotate meat 2-3 times to saturate evenly.

### Pinquito Beans[73]
1lb pinquito beans (2c dry)
2-3 cloves of garlic (or 1Tbl minced)
1 large onion, chopped
1 green pepper, chopped
1Tbl chili powder

[72] For an interesting variation try kiwi instead of citrus juice. I add the soy sauce to a blender and drop in 2 or 3 peeled and sliced kiwis. Give it a buzz and mix in the other ingredients. Kiwi is a natural meat tenderizer and you may be surprised. It really works!
[73] If you can't find these beans, you can order them from: Lompoc Warehouse Corp., 1119 W. Laurel Ave., Lompoc, CA. 93436. (805) 736-2517.

1/4tsp cumin powder
salt and pepper to taste
1/2lb pork chorizo (or hamburger, ham or pork sausage)
1c salsa (or tomato sauce)

Wash and pick over beans. Soak in a large pot or Dutch oven in cold water overnight. Drain and add fresh water about 2 inches above the level of the beans. Add minced garlic, onion, pepper and spices. If you use chorizo, you may not need the chili powder. Cook until beans are tender. In a skillet, brown chorizo, then add to beans along with salsa. Serves 6-8.

## JUNE'S SALSA
29oz canned "Mexican Style" stewed tomatoes
4oz can diced green chilies
2oz can jalapeños, diced (optional)
1 bunch of green onions, finely chopped
1/2 bunch fresh cilantro, chopped
pepper, oregano and garlic powder (not garlic salt) to taste

Place stewed tomatoes in a blender and chop for 2-3 seconds. Transfer to a medium mixing bowl and combine with remaining ingredients. If you want to crank up the heat a notch, add diced jalapeños. Hint: A tablespoon of olive oil will help to preserve the salsa, if needed.

## TOSSED GREEN SALAD
1 cucumber, thinly sliced
1 carrot, grated
1/2 red onion, thinly sliced
2 tomatoes cut into small wedges
2 heads green lettuce (bibb or romaine), chopped or torn
1 avocado, sliced (reserve for topping the salad)

This salad can be tossed with another local favorite, now served nationwide; Hidden Valley® Original Ranch® Dressing. This dressing was developed by a real rancher at a real ranch back in the early 1960s—the Hidden Valley Guest Ranch on San Marcos Pass overlooking Santa Barbara, California. If you prefer, you can toss it with some Susie Q's or lemon pepper, the juice of a fresh lemon and a little extra virgin olive oil.

## GARLIC BREAD

1Tbl fresh crushed garlic
1/2tsp paprika
1/4c soft butter
1/4c mayonnaise
1 loaf Sourdough,[74] French or Italian bread
Santa Maria Style Seasoning or garlic salt to taste
1c fine shredded fresh Romano cheese (optional)

Mix crushed garlic and paprika into the soft butter and mayonnaise and spread on both sides of a loaf of sliced bread. You can toast the bread on the grill: wrap in Aluminum foil and bake for 10 minutes at 350F or broil until golden brown. If you grill or broil the bread, you will have to stand there and watch it or the bread will burn. Close bread sides and slice crosswise into 1-1/2" slices.

## FRESH STRAWBERRY GLAZE PIE

1c sugar
6Tbl cornstarch
3oz package Strawberry Jell-O
2c water
2qt fresh strawberries, hulled
2 9-inch baked pie shells

In a saucepan, combine sugar, cornstarch, Jell-O and water. Cook over medium heat, stirring constantly, until the mixture thickens; let it come to a boil. Boil for 1 minute stirring constantly. Remove from heat and set aside to cool.

Fill crusts with whole or cut strawberries. Pour cooked strawberry glaze over the fresh strawberries. Refrigerate for 3 hours, or until set. Serve with Cool Whip or lightly sweetened whipped cream. Makes 12 servings.

---

[74] Locals like San Luis Sourdough. See www.slodough.com for retail locations.

## More BBQ

### STEAKS

The main thing to remember about steaks is to use choice or prime grade beef only. Stay away from "select" grade beef sold in most supermarkets. As good as the following marinade is, it will not turn a bad steak into a good steak.

I love T-bones, Porterhouse, New York Strip and Rib Eye steaks. My favorite, however, has got to be the Rib Eye. If I'm really in the mood for a good steak, I'll go to a meat market and buy a half Prime Rib Roast with ribs attached. When I get it home, I remove the ribs, trim the rib "eye" and cut it into 1-1/4" to 1-1/2" steaks.

Place steaks in 1gal zip lock bags with enough marinade to cover and let them sit overnight or at least 4 hours in the refrigerator. Grill steaks for 6-8 minutes per side for medium rare to medium.

#### MARINADE FOR STEAKS
2c red wine (or apple cider vinegar)
1c tomato sauce
1/2c brown sugar
1/4c Worcestershire Sauce
1/4c prepared mustard
1tsp Tabasco
1Tbl salt
1Tbl black pepper
3-4 whole cloves of garlic, crushed

Combine ingredients in a blender. Transfer to a 3qt saucepan, bring to a slow rolling boil and cook for 15 min. Let cool at least to room temperature or refrigerate before using.

#### KIELBASA WITH STIR-FRIED VEGETABLES
2 zucchini
2 onions
1 green bell pepper
1 red bell pepper
2Tbl olive oil
2Tbl vinegar
1lb Smoked Turkey Kielbasa (or any style Kielbasa)
salt and pepper to taste

Chop or thick slice vegetables and place in a medium mixing bowl. Add oil and toss, coating vegetables thoroughly. Add vinegar, salt and pepper, and toss again. Preheat BBQ Wok on grill. Divide Kielbasa in two and place on either side of wok. Spray wok (or a vegetable grate designed for the grill) then add vegetables and stir-fry until tender crisp.

Serve with sweet hot mustard dipping sauce. Sometimes I mix equal parts of prepared mustard, Teriyaki (or Soy) Sauce and honey.

## CHICKEN POPPERS

1lb sliced bacon (regular thickness)
7oz can whole green chilies
2lb boneless skinless chicken thighs
Teriyaki Sauce (optional)

This is really simple, somewhat tedious, but awesomely delicious! The bacon should have about 16 slices in a package. Slice the slab down the middle and separate slices, forming 32 halves for rolling the chilies and thigh pieces. Remove whole chilies from the can and slice open. Then slice each chilies into six pieces about the size of the end of your thumb. Take thigh meat and slice into chunks about the size and thickness of the end of your thumb. Hopefully you will have at least 32 chunks of thigh meat and 32 chili slices to go with the bacon strips.

Lay a bacon strip out flat. Place a piece of green chili at one end and a chunk of thigh meat on top. Roll it up and skewer it. Repeat process placing 6-8 poppers on each skewer. Grill on the "Barby" turning occasionally for even doneness. The bacon provides plenty of salt for taste, but you can baste with Teriyaki Sauce if desired to add a little sweetness.

## CORN ON THE COB

Surprisingly, corn on the cob tastes sweeter to me if the fresh ears are frozen before they are cooked. Remove shucks and silk, rinse and freeze in a large freezer bag. Place several frozen ears into a large pot of boiling water. Let them steep for about 10 minutes, then serve with butter, salt and pepper.

The other way, of course is to cook them on the BBQ. I've seen it done two different ways. Grilling them with the "shucks on" is a little messy, but protects the corn from burning and drying out. First, peel back the shucks, but don't remove them. Remove the "silk," rinse the ears in water, then fold the shucks back over the ears. Secure them with twine. Grill for about 30 minutes. Turn them occasionally while grilling. They should turn out moist and flavorful.

Yet another other way is to grill them already shucked. This too, can be very tasty if the heat is well-regulated and you can keep from burning the ears or drying them out too much.

## CALICO BEANS

1/2lb bacon, chopped
2-15oz cans kidney beans
2-16oz cans Pork 'n Beans
2-15oz cans butter beans
1 onion, chopped
1/2c ketchup
1/4c brown sugar
1/4c vinegar
2Tbl prepared mustard
1/2lb ground beef (or ground turkey)

Chop bacon into bite-size pieces and brown in a cast-iron skillet. Meanwhile add beans to a large pot or Dutch oven. Reserve liquid and add later as needed. When bacon is done, transfer to beans and sauté chopped onion in bacon drippings. Meanwhile, combine ketchup, brown sugar, vinegar and mustard in a mixing bowl and add to beans. Transfer sautéed onion to beans, then brown ground beef in a skillet and add to the beans. Add just enough reserved liquid to make the pot of beans easy to stir. Heat and serve.

## STRAWBERRY AND RED ONION SALAD

1qt fresh strawberries, hulled
1 large red onion, thinly sliced into rings
3 hearts of romaine lettuce, chopped

Fresh strawberries can be left whole or they can be halved. Toss ingredients in a large mixing bowl. Transfer to salad bowl and serve with Poppy Seed dressing.

# Dinner on the Grounds

As a kid growing up at Trinity Baptist Church in McAlester, Oklahoma, I can remember occasional summer get-togethers for food, fun and fellowship. Dinner on the Grounds! We literally spread out blankets on the grounds next to the Church and had picnics: fried chicken, fried okra, coleslaw, chocolate cake and, of course, homemade ice cream.

We used the old "hand-crank" wooden bucket ice cream freezers, and guess who always got stuck with the crankin'? That's right, the young boys. I didn't lift weights as a teenager, but crankin' ice cream built up my biceps. It was worth the effort, believe me.

I asked my brother Owen once what foods made him think of Daddy. With little hesitation, he said, "Ice Cream." That's what I was thinking too, but waited to see if his remembrance was the same as mine.

*Trinity Baptist Church*
*McAlester, Oklahoma*
*Founded June 18, 1950*
*Last Sunday Service Nov. 21, 2004*

## HOMEMADE PEACH ICE CREAM

2c fresh peaches
32fl oz Half-and-Half
16oz whipping cream (or canned evaporated milk)
1-3/4c sugar
3oz package Jell-O Instant Vanilla Pudding (optional)
1tsp almond extract
1tsp vanilla extract
1/2tsp salt

Use fresh peaches. Do not use canned peaches! Peel peaches, remove the stone (pit) and dice into very small chunks (or puree in a food processor). Combine half-and-half, whipping cream, sugar, pudding mix, almond and vanilla extract and salt. Add peaches and mix thoroughly. Transfer to ice cream container and prepare according to the ice cream maker's instructions. Makes 2 quarts. These days, I recommend an electric ice cream maker.

## HOMEMADE VANILLA ICE CREAM

48fl oz Half-and-Half
16fl oz whipping cream (or canned evaporated milk)
2c sugar
3oz package Jell-O instant Vanilla Pudding (optional)
2tsp vanilla extract
1/2tsp salt

Combine half-and-half, whipping cream, sugar, pudding mix, vanilla extract and salt. Transfer to ice cream container and prepare according to the ice cream maker's instructions. Makes 2 quarts.

## *The Memorial Service of O. J. Finley, Jr.*

My kids have their own memories of my father, and Janni and I have ours. I'm so grateful that we were all able to attend his funeral in Nashville in the late winter of 2003. Truly his life and dedication to his sacred calling have molded our lives as much as any other force or influence to come our way.

I don't think I could do a better job of recalling my father's character and life achievements than my brother Howard's eulogy at the funeral service. I still feel Daddy's presence in my life, sometimes more powerfully now than when he walked this earth. I want to please him. I want to honor him. And I want to be with him in heaven forever.

### A Eulogy by Howard Paul Finley
### Delivered on March 1, 2003

Thank you Pastor Cruise, and all the faithful members of Belmont Heights Baptist Church: (Nashville, Tennesse)

On behalf of my mother, Fanneita Finley and my brothers Owen and John, as well as all the members of our family, I want to thank you for gathering here in this place to pay your respects and honor the life of my Dad, a husband, a father and a grandfather; but above all else, a Christian.

James Barry (Dad's Sunday School Teacher) asked that one of the family members share a remembrance of our father's pastoral ministry in McAlester, Oklahoma. If you knew my dad at all, you'd know he did not like to speak of himself in terms of his work as a pastor, his accomplishments and especially his wartime experiences. Dad wanted to talk about Christ, the Scriptures and the Church. Dad was most keenly interested in what he and others could be doing right now to proclaim the Gospel of Christ—and he did it. No one who encountered my father, whether it be at his apartment complex, the laundromat, Krogers, the pharmacy, a restaurant or a waiting room failed to learn, in a gentle way, that he was a committed Christian.

As my brothers and I reflected on his ministry in Oklahoma, it was impossible to do so without recognizing the impact of the events of the Normandy Invasion of the Second World War on his life and work. When Dad retired and was giving his last sermon at Trinity Baptist Church in McAlester, Oklahoma, he made a rare, dramatic and very brief mention of the events that transpired. He said, "As a young second lieutenant, early in the morning on June the 6th, 1944, I went over the side of a destroyer into a small landing craft as part of the invasion of Normandy. As we landed, I and others kicked down the door of that craft and hit the sands of Omaha Beach—and four days later—boom— my whole life was changed." My Dad's life was changed spiritually.

You see, it took my Dad and his comrades most of the day to reach the tops of the Cliffs at Normandy. The first wave at his point of entry had been unsuccessful in its efforts to take the beach. He was unable ever to describe the horror of it all. He did once say that many of those men who went before him never even made it to the sand.[75]

A few of the things he said were: that the air attack seemed to have failed. "We were just being slaughtered by German 88s, mortars and German Sharp Shooters." He was pinned down in a tide pool for a while when a veteran of the North Africa Campaign noticed mortars hitting in the water right behind. "They've got us in their sights," he said. "We have got to make a run for it." My Dad and those with him did run; eight steps pitch and roll, eight steps pitch and roll (a drill designed to keep you out of the enemy's gun sight when running). He once told me that the men who didn't keep moving did not make it.

At the base of the cliffs they located a tape line leading upward through a ravine to the top— someone had made it up, and they followed that line to a point where they could continue to fight from cover. I don't know much about the second and third days. He did mention witnessing an unimaginable air attack in the night and being sent out alone in the hedge rows of France to identify possible staging areas for vehicles and supply. He also said there was lots of confusion—men separated from their units, so many officers killed that logistics were just a matter of doing what you had to do, remembering and reminding yourself of your mission.

Sometime on or before June 10th, as they were preparing to enter one of the small coastal villages, he was approached by, I think he said a major, who ordered him back to the beach. "Are you a second lieutenant?" He said, "Yes sir." "I want you you to go back to the beach with these

---

[75] These were the soldiers of the 16th Infantry Regiment of the 1st Infantry Division in the first wave at Omaha Beach. Daddy was in the second wave with the 20th Engineer (C) Battalion that landed in their assault echelon. For its efforts on Omaha Beach, the battalion was awarded the Presidential Unit Citation and the French Croix de Guerre. Daddy also received a Europe-North African-Middle Eastern Theater Ribbon, one battle star and a purple heart.

The 20th Engineer Battalion went on to fight across France, Belgium and Germany with many different divisions in battles such as the Hurtgen Forest and Battle of the Bulge, and ended the war in Czechoslovakia.
Ref. www.globalsecurity.org/military/agency/army/20eng.htm and www.20thengineerbattalion.org/
see: Content/Unit Histories/20th Engineer Battalion/World War II.

forty men and search for snipers, they are still shooting at our guys down there." Even though my Dad was not well trained for combat (he was a combat engineer) he said, "You didn't argue, you obeyed the order."

American soldiers leave Coast Guard landing boats under heavy Nazi machine gun fire. (National Archives)

In a possible first encounter with a sniper, my dad traversed a barbed wire fence and moved forward, alone, to establish his leadership with the men. A few yards out, he stepped on a land mine severely wounding his right leg, arm and side. The medic and four others went in after him. While carrying him out on a stretcher, one of them stepped on a second mine. Three were killed instantly, the medic survived, and my dad's legs took another blast. Somehow he remained conscious through it all.

Time would prevent me from going further, but it was in that bloody field that O.J. Finley, Jr. was spiritually changed. He beseeched God to spare his life, to let him walk, and he promised to serve Him. Dad once told us, "Because others had died for me, I could no longer live for myself, I felt I had to live for others."

And live for others he did. My brothers and I would like you to know five aspects of the character of his ministry. First of all, Dad was a man of prayer and personal devotion to the scriptures. He prayed on his knees three times a day as long a I knew him right up to his first stroke, and I am 47 years old. From 1998 (after my return to Nashville) until May of 2001 when he was first stricken, there must have been at least a couple of dozen times when I walked into Dad's apartment on Woodmont Boulevard, unannounced, and he was on his knees in prayer. At Wednesday Night Bible Study at Trinity Baptist in McAlester,Oklahoma, he, and even the congregation would kneel for intercessory prayer time.

He prayed for literally hundreds of people. Some of you may have seen him pull a little spiral notepad out of his shirt pocket and make a note. It was your name, a son or daughter's name, a birthday, an anniversary. This would be transferred to scores of lists he maintained, and he would pray for you. He prayed for no one more than his sons, their wives and his grandchildren.

Second, he had a gift for comforting the sick and the grief-stricken. Hospital visits were a regular part of his weekly routine. He was sensitive to anyone's suffering because of his own. He did not just visit members of his church, but anyone he knew and anyone who asked. Because he dwelt in his same, small hometown until his retirement in 1989, he knew everyone. He probably holds some kind of record for funerals conducted, because he knew so many and he

*Owen Jefferson Finley, Jr.*
*my father*
*b. Oct. 12, 1922 d. Feb. 28, 2003*

had a special ability to capture a person's life, to console and to deliver that life and consolation in a sermon. The local funeral homes always called on Pastor Finley for families in need of someone to conduct a final memorial.

Third, Dad was a good preacher and teacher, but most of all a pastor. He remained in that same small church, one pastorate, for 38 years, choosing to cultivate a small vineyard rather than move up to larger churches. He seemed to have no regard for advancement in this life. He could have moved, and had been approached on occasion, but he never felt called of the Lord to make a change. A congregation has to love you to keep you for so long. I recall a woman at his retirement banquet saying, "We have always been so proud to have Brother Finley as our pastor, we knew he would never do anything to embarrass us."

*Bless the Lord, O my soul: and all that is within me, bless his holy name.[76] Bless the Lord, O my soul, and forget not all his benefits: Who forgiveth all thine iniquities; who healeth all thy diseases; Who redeemeth thy life from destruction; who crowneth thee with lovingkindness and tender mercies; Who satisfieth thy youth with good things; so that thy youth is renewed like the eagle's.*

*The Lord executeth righteousness and judgment for all that are oppressed. He made known his ways unto Moses, his acts unto the children of Israel. The Lord is merciful and gracious, slow to anger, and plenteous in mercy. He will not always chide: neither will he keep his anger forever. He hath not dealt with us after our sins; nor rewarded us according to our iniquities. For as the heaven is high above the earth, so great is his mercy toward them that fear him. As far as the east is from the west, so far hath he removed our transgressions from us. Like as a father pitieth his children, so the Lord pitieth them that fear him. For he knoweth our frame; he remembereth that we are dust.*

*As for man, his days are as grass; as a flower of the field, so he flourisheth. For the wind passeth over it, and it is gone; and the place thereof shall know it no more. But the mercy of the Lord is from everlasting to everlasting upon them that fear him, and his righteousness unto children's children; To such as keep his covenant, and to those that remember his commandments to do them.*

*The Lord hath prepared his throne in the heavens; and his kingdom ruleth over all.*

*Bless the Lord, ye his angels, that excel in strength, that do his commmandments, hearkening unto the voice of his word. Bless ye the Lord, all ye his hosts; ye ministers of his, that do his pleasure. Bless the Lord, all his works in all places of his dominion: bless the Lord, O my soul.[157]* Psalm 102(103)

---

[76] Daddy would always quote this verse when someone joined the Church at Trinity Baptist.

Fourth, although loyal to the Southern Baptist Denomination and the tenets of the Baptist Faith and message, he was a leader amongst the other Christian ministers in the Ministerial Alliance of McAlester, Oklahoma. Together they developed a local radio broadcast and published weekly articles in the local newspapers entitled "Manna." In anyone's absence or illness, Dad would usually be the one to cover the radio show or the article. My brother Owen recalls stopping at a store on a hunting trip with our grandfather, and the owners "going on" about how much they enjoyed hearing Dad speak on the radio.

Fifth, the war and the very positive influences of his parents made Dad a staunch supporter of equality among the races. He once told my brother John, "After the war, we could not come back to America as it had been. We had fought together with African Americans against the most racist regime in history." In seminary, where he and my mother earned Masters Degrees, Mom and Dad chose to do all their field ministry developing churches and programs among the National Baptists and Missionary Baptist Churches of the African American community there in Louisville, Kentucky. In McAlester, he conducted joint services between the East Star Baptist Church, an African American church, and Trinity Baptist. My brother Owen recalled how Dad would take the children of his church over to East Star Baptist to see what their children had made in Vacation Bible School and then their pastor would bring his Vacation Bible School over to see what we had done.

When Martin Luther King, Jr. was shot, my dad stood hand in hand with the Black Community to memorialize his life. Dad did this with little or no support from the community and sometimes, even with some silent criticism from those close to him.

On a final note, my Mother stood by Dad in everything, she played a key role in his ultimate recovery from the wounds of war and was likewise called into the ministry. Mom was instrumental in every success my father experienced.

There is so much more that could be said, but I simply want to close my remarks by giving thanks to God for a life lived well and for an example which, with the help of the Father, Son and Holy Spirit, will continue on in our family for many generations. Thank you.

CHAPTER 7 ~ *More Family Favorites*

## *Grandma Morrison's Recipes*

Janni's mother Phyllis Morrison moved her family to Goleta, California in 1970, shortly after her husband (Janni's father) was tragically killed in an automobile accident in Washington State. Phyllis diligently provided for her four children while teaching school full-time. Although she has never gotten involved with fancy entertaining, she has cooked for a lot of people over the years and still enjoys making a few of her favorites on special occasions.

Phyllis has been living with our family for the past 13 years. Her faith in God and love for her family displayed in manifold ways has been a tremendous inspiration to her children and to her children's children. Her blessing has now come to yet another generation with the birth of her great-granddaughter, Atalia Finley.

*Phyllis Gish Morrison*

### CHILI-CHEESE APPETIZERS
1/2c butter
10 eggs, beaten
1/2c flour
1tsp baking powder
dash of salt
4oz can chopped green chilies
16oz cottage cheese
1lb Jack cheese, grated

Melt butter in a 9x13 pan. Beat eggs lightly in a large bowl. Add flour, baking powder and a dash of salt. Add melted butter, chilies, cottage cheese and grated Jack cheese. Mix only until blended. Pour into the buttered pan and bake at 400F for 15 minutes. Reduce heat to 350F and bake for an additional 35-40 minutes. Cut into squares and serve.

*Note: Squares may be frozen, then thawed and reheated a few at a time.*

## POTATO SALAD

12 hard-boiled eggs
5lb red or russet potatoes
rice vinegar
2c celery, finely chopped
2 bunches green onions, chopped
dill pickles, chopped (optional)
radishes, chopped (optional)
2c mayonnaise
mustard (a few squirts)
a little dill pickle juice
2tsp sugar
celery salt, seasoned salt, seasoned pepper, garlic powder, and dill weed to taste
paprika (for color and decoration)

Hard boil eggs. In a large Dutch oven, boil whole potatoes for 25 minutes. Test and remove small cooked potatoes and set aside. Gradually remove all potatoes as they are done. They should be soft enough to pierce with a fork, but not mushy. When cooled, slice potatoes into 1/2" cubes. Toss with rice vinegar and refrigerate overnight.

The next day, slice 10 eggs both ways in an egg slicer and combine with potatoes in a large mixing bowl. Add celery and onions. In a separate bowl, combine mayonnaise, a few squirts of mustard, pickle juice, sugar and spices. Pour over potato salad and gently stir. Add more salt, pepper or dill to taste. Transfer potato salad to a serving bowl. Slice two remaining eggs; decorate top and sprinkle with paprika.

## JELL-O SALAD

2 20oz cans, crushed pineapple (in its own juice)
6oz package Raspberry Jell-O
2lb low-fat cottage cheese
1lb Lite Cool Whip whipped topping

Pour off just a little juice from the top of each can. Transfer to a large pan and bring crushed pineapple to a boil in its own juice. Remove from heat, transfer to a mixing bowl and gradually stir in package of Jell-O. Refrigerate overnight. The next day, fold in cottage cheese and Cool Whip. Serves 12 as a side salad or for dessert. Grandma likes to eat it for breakfast!

## CHICKEN AND RICE CASSEROLE

1c long-grain rice
1pkg dry onion soup mix
1c water
1 frying chicken, skinned and cut up
10oz can condensed cream of mushroom soup

Grease a 9x13 baking dish and preheat oven to 350F. Spread uncooked rice in dish. Sprinkle with 1/2 package onion soup and add water. Lay chicken parts over rice. Sprinkle with rest of soup mix. Pour mushroom soup over all and cover with foil. Bake 60-75 minutes.

## CHICKEN BROCCOLI CASSEROLE

5 boneless chicken breasts
1-1/2lb fresh broccoli
2 cans cream of mushroom soup
3/4c mayonnaise
1/4c lemon juice
1 bunch green onions, chopped
lemon pepper to taste
2c grated cheddar cheese
2.8oz can fried onion rings

There are four layers to the casserole: broccoli, chicken mixture, cheese and fried onion rings.

Place chicken breasts in a 9x13 baking dish. Cover with foil and bake in oven at 350F for one hour. Remove from oven, drain off stock, remove from baking dish and let cool. Parboil broccoli in a Dutch oven for 5 minutes and remove. Chop and add to 9x13 baking dish. In a medium mixing bowl, add cream of mushroom soup, mayonnaise, lemon juice and chopped green onions, sprinkle with lemon pepper and stir. Dice chicken and add to creamy mixture. Pour over broccoli in baking dish, sprinkle with grated cheese, top with onion rings, cover with foil and bake at 350F for 30 minutes.

## BLACK BEAN SOUP

1lb dry black beans, soaked overnight
8-9c chicken stock
2c onion, diced
2c celery, diced
1c carrot, diced
4oz can diced green chilies
3 large cloves of garlic, minced
cumin to taste
1/4c tamari (or soy sauce)
sea salt to taste

Soak 1lb dry black beans for 8 hours or overnight. Drain beans and discard water. Add chicken stock to beans and bring to a boil. Add onions, celery, carrots and minced garlic. Reduce heat and simmer for about 45 minutes. Beans and vegetables should be slightly tender. Add green chilies, cumin to taste and tamari, and simmer 15 minutes. Ladle about one cup of soup and puree in a blender, then add back to soup. Salt (or add more tamari) to taste.

## APPLE CRANBERRY CRISP

8c Granny Smith or Braeburn apples (approx 3 lb), peeled, cored and thinly sliced
16oz can whole cranberry sauce
1/3c brown sugar, firmly packed
3Tbl all-purpose flour
2tsp cinnamon
1c chopped walnuts (optional)

### TOPPING

2/3c brown sugar, firmly packed
3/4c old-fashioned oats
1tsp nutmeg
3/4c all-purpose flour
2tsp cinnamon
1/2c softened butter or margarine
1/4c water
1/4tsp salt

Preheat oven to 350F. Slice apples and place in a 9x13 casserole (a stone baking dish is ideal). In a small bowl, combine cranberry sauce, sugar, flour and cinnamon. Mix well. Pour over sliced apples and stir to blend. Set aside. If using walnuts, top apples with walnut pieces. Mix topping ingredients in a bowl with a pastry blender. Sprinkle over apples. Bake 40-45 minutes or until apples are tender and top is golden brown. Makes 6-8 servings.

### KORRUPSU (GERMAN PANCAKE)
2Tbl butter
3 eggs
2-1/2c milk
1c flour
1/3c sugar
1/2tsp salt
1tsp vanilla extract (if desired)
cinnamon and more sugar

Melt butter in a 9x13 baking dish. Mix eggs, milk, flour, sugar, salt and vanilla in a blender. Bake at 375F for 35-40 minutes. Mixture should be brown on top and pulling away from the sides. Sprinkle with cinnamon and sugar. Serve hot!

## *Some of My Wife's Favorites*

### COUNTRY FRENCH VEGETABLE SOUP
3 carrots, thinly sliced
3 medium (or 2 large) potatoes, cubed
2 14.5oz cans chicken broth
1c water
salt and pepper to taste
8oz can tomato sauce
1/4c fresh parsley, finely chopped
1/4c butter
3 shallots, finely chopped
2 cloves garlic, minced
10oz package frozen peas (or 15oz can Le Sueur peas, drained)

In a large saucepan or soup pot, cook together the first seven ingredients and simmer mixture for 45 minutes or until vegetables are tender. Do not cover the soup pot entirely, but leave the lid slightly ajar.

Meanwhile, sauté together the remaining ingredients until the shallots are tender. Add this mixture, along with the peas, to the soup pot and continue simmering for 15 minutes. Divide mixture between 6-8 ovenproof bowls. Float a slice of French bread with garlic Swiss cheese on top and broil for a few seconds until the cheese is lightly browned. Serves 6-8.

### PEAR, WALNUT AND GORGONZOLA SALAD
Dressing
3Tbl powdered (confectioner's) sugar
1tsp dry mustard
1/2tsp sea salt
2Tbl white vinegar
1/4c canola oil

Mix the first four dressing ingredients together in a bowl. Using a hand mixer on high speed or a wire whisk, slowly drizzle the oil into the dressing until it is the consistency of honey.

2 pears, cored and thinly sliced
juice of 1/2 lemon
1/2c walnuts (whole or pieces), toasted
12oz mixed salad greens
1/2c crumbled Gorgonzola cheese

To keep the peeled pears from turning brown, slice them into a small bowl with water and the juice of 1/2 lemon added to it. Drain liquid from slices just before use. Spread walnuts evenly in the bottom of a bread pan and toast at 400F for about 10 minutes.

Combine pears and greens in a large salad bowl. Pour the dressing over the greens and mix thoroughly. Add walnuts, cheese and toss again. Serve immediately. Serves 4-6.

### CHINESE CABBAGE SALAD
3/4c slivered almonds, toasted
1 medium head napa (Chinese) cabbage, thinly sliced
1 bunch green onions, chopped
1/2c snow pea pods (optional)
1 package Top Ramen noodles

#### SALAD DRESSING
1/4c canola (or salad) oil
1Tbl sesame oil

3Tbl brown sugar
2Tbl rice vinegar
1Tbl soy sauce
2Tbl sesame seeds, toasted
1 Ramen flavor packet

In a bread pan, toast almonds and sesame seeds for 10 minutes at 350F. (If you bought toasted sesame seeds, don't toast them again.) Meanwhile, thinly slice cabbage and chop onions. In a large mixing bowl, toss cabbage, onions, snow pea pods and almonds. Combine ingredients for dressing, add to salad and toss again. Just before serving, break up Ramen noodles and add to cabbage salad. Toss lightly and serve. Serves 4.

## SHRIMP PASTA SALAD
1lb frozen cooked shrimp
1c lemon juice
1lb rotini (curly) noodles
1lb fresh broccoli
1/2 red onion, chopped
2oz jar diced pimientos, drained
4oz jar capers, drained
3.8oz sliced black olives (1/2c)
5oz whole Spanish olives (1c)
1/2c extra virgin olive oil
1/4c soy sauce

Soak shrimp overnight in lemon juice. Cook noodles in boiling salted water for 8-10 minutes. Rinse and drain with cold water. Blanch broccoli for 5 minutes. Peel rough layer off broccoli and chop stems. Leave flowerets whole. Place in a large mixing bowl. Dice red onion and add to broccoli. Drain pimientos, capers, olives and shrimp. Discard lemon juice.

In a large mixing bowl, combine with all ingredients (except olive oil and soy sauce) and toss lightly. Combine extra virgin olive and soy sauce in a large measuring cup. Whisk thoroughly, then pour over combined ingredients. Toss lightly again. Transfer to a serving bowl and refrigerate until cool. Makes 6-8 servings.

## RICE-A-RONI SALAD
2 boxes Chicken Rice-a-Roni, cooked and cooled
1 bunch green onions, chopped
4 small jars marinated artichoke hearts, drained and cut up (save juice)

2 green peppers, chopped
1/2c mayonnaise
juice from artichoke heart jars
1/2tsp curry powder
2tsp dry mustard

Prepare Rice-a-Roni in advance according to package directions.

*Note: You may not need all the juice from the artichoke heart jars.*
*The salad needs to be moist, but not soupy.*

Combine and mix all ingredients. Transfer to a serving bowl and chill overnight.

## Special Breads

### BANANA BREAD
3-1/2c flour
1tsp soda
1tsp salt
1Tbl cream of tartar
1c vegetable shortening
1-1/3c sugar
4 eggs, well beaten
2c (4-5) ripe bananas, mashed

Mix flour, soda, salt and cream of tartar in mixing bowl. In a separate bowl, cream shortening; add sugar a little at a time and stir until light and fluffy. Add eggs and beat well. Add flour mixture alternately with bananas, a small amount at a time and beat after each addition until smooth. Pour mixture evenly into 2 well-greased loaf pans and bake in 325 oven for 55-60 minutes.

### PERSIMMON BREAD
2c persimmon pulp (pureed) from 3 large persimmons
4c flour
1-3/4c brown sugar
1/2c margarine or butter, melted

1/4c vinegar
1Tbl baking soda
2tsp salt
1tsp cinnamon
1tsp nutmeg
1/2tsp ground cloves (or allspice)
1c chopped pecans (optional)
1c seedless golden raisins (optional)

Slice persimmons (the softer the better),[77] core the hard middle and blend them in a food processor. It is not necessary to peel them although you may want to cut out any hard or discolored areas on the skin. Transfer puree to a medium mixing bowl, add remaining ingredients and mix thoroughly. Spoon mixture evenly into 2 well-greased loaf pans and bake at 325F for 70 minutes.

## My Mother's Dishes

My mother was a very practical cook—nothing fancy, no special recipes. None of what follows is original. She collected a few favorites though and made them occasionally. Here are a 0number of dishes that remind me of her.

*Our two-bedroom, one-bath house on S. 14th Street in McAlester, Oklahoma*

### CARROT CAKE
4 eggs, beaten
1c all-vegetable shortening (or canola oil)
3/4c buttermilk
2c sugar
2tsp vanilla extract
2c flour
2tsp baking soda
2tsp cinnamon
1tsp salt
2-1/2c carrots grated (approx. 1 lb)

[77] Persimmons really need a good frost to fully ripen. In Santa Barbara that's not likely to happen, so I like to put them in the freezer overnight (or longer) and pull them out as needed for this recipe.

1c chopped nuts
1 small can crushed pineapple, thoroughly drained

In a medium mixing bowl blend eggs, oil, buttermilk, sugar and vanilla extract. Sift in flour, and add baking soda, cinnamon and salt. Blend ingredients with a mixer, then add carrots, nuts and pineapple, and mix thoroughly by hand. Pour into 2 greased and lightly floured 9x1-1/2-inch round pans and bake at 350F for 35 minutes or until done. Cool for 10 minutes before removing from pans onto a cooling rack.

### FROSTING
1 cube (1/2c) butter or margarine
8oz package cream cheese
1lb box powdered sugar

Blend ingredients with mixer and frost cake after it has cooled thoroughly.

## CHIPPED BEEF ON TOAST
5oz HORMEL® dried beef, chopped (packages or jars)
1/4c butter or margarine
1/4c flour
2-2/3c milk
1tsp Worcestershire sauce
a few dashes of pepper
6 toast points

In a skillet, cook dried beef in butter for a few minutes. Stir flour into butter mixture; add milk. Cook and stir until thickened and bubbly. Stir in Worcestershire Sauce and pepper. Cook and stir 2-3 minutes longer. Spoon over toast. Makes 6 servings.

## TUNA CASSEROLE
3/4c rice
2c chicken broth or water
2 12oz cans albacore tuna, drained
15oz can sweet peas, drained
1 large onion, chopped
8oz sour cream or IMO (sour cream substitute)
lemon pepper and dill weed to taste
1/2c bread or cracker crumbs

2Tbl canola oil

8oz can water chestnuts, drained and chopped (optional)

Simmer rice in chicken broth or water for 20 minutes. Flake tuna in a medium mixing bowl. Add peas, chopped onion, sour cream (or IMO), lemon pepper and dill weed. In a small bowl, mix bread crumbs with canola oil. Finally, add cooked rice to tuna mixture and mix thoroughly. Transfer to a 9x9 casserole dish and top with bread crumbs. Bake at 350F for 40 minutes.

## HAM, PEA AND CHEESE SALAD

1c chopped red onion

1/4tsp salt

1/4c mayonnaise

2Tbl chopped sweet pickle, drained

1Tbl prepared mustard

1c cubed Swiss cheese (4oz)

2c cubed cooked ham (1/2lb)

16oz frozen early harvest petite peas, thawed

4-6 large lettuce leaves

In a medium mixing bowl, thoroughly combine onion, salt, mayonnaise, pickle and mustard. Add cheese, ham and peas and toss lightly. Chill until serving time. Serve mounded on lettuce leaves. Serves 4-6.

## MEAT LOAF

1-1/2lb ground beef[78] (no more than 15% fat)

1 egg, beaten

1c salsa

1c oats

1 medium onion, finely chopped

1 large carrot, grated

Mix ground meat, egg and salsa by hand thoroughly in a large mixing bowl. I mean use your hand instead of a fork or spoon. It'll make you feel like a real cook! Add oats, chopped onion, and grated carrot and repeat the process. Transfer to a bread-baking pan and cook at 350F for 1 hour.

For a variation, use ground turkey instead of ground beef and a 4oz jar of chopped pimientos instead of salsa.

[78] If you can find some lean ground pork, try using 3/4lb ground pork and 3/4lb ground beef in combination.

Mother collected a number of recipes from her friend in McAlester, Lahoma Whitson. Here are two of my favorites:

## MRS. WHITSON'S SQUASH CASSEROLE

10-3/4oz can cream of chicken soup concentrate
1 medium onion, chopped
8oz can water chestnuts, drained and sliced
8oz light sour cream
1 large egg, beaten
6c summer squash, sliced thin
1/2tsp marjoram or poultry seasoning (optional)
1/4c margarine (or canola oil)
1c bread crumbs

In a large mixing bowl, combine cream of chicken soup concentrate, onion, water chestnuts, sour cream and an egg. Add sliced squash and mix well. Melt margarine and mix with bread crumbs. Lightly grease a 9x13 casserole. Add squash mixture and top with bread crumbs. Bake at 375F for 40 minutes.

*Note: Casserole will freeze well before baking. Make sure it is completely thawed, however, before baking.*

## MRS. WHITSON'S CHOCOLATE CAKE

2c all-purpose flour
2c granulated sugar
1c water
1/2c Crisco oil
1 stick, Parkay margarine (1/2c)
3Tbl cocoa
2 eggs
1/2c buttermilk
1tsp soda
1/8tsp salt
1-2tsp vanilla extract

In a large mixing bowl add flour and sugar and mix by hand. In a medium saucepan add water, Crisco oil, margarine and cocoa. Bring just to a boil. Pour over flour and sugar mixture and mix well. Add eggs, buttermilk, soda, salt and vanilla extract and mix well by hand (Don't use a mixer). Batter will be thin.

Bake in a large floured cake pan (at least 9x13). Bake at 350F for 30 minutes in a gas oven or 20-25 in an electric oven. (Since ovens vary, check the cake after 20 minutes in either oven.)

### Icing
1/3c milk
1/4c margarine, melted
1Tbl vanilla extract
2-3Tbl cocoa
powdered sugar

Combine milk, melted margarine, vanilla extract and cocoa. Add powdered sugar to the desired thickness you like. Spread on cake while it's hot and enjoy!

## *A Life of Sacrifice*

As I write these words, my mother is in an assisted living facility in Nashville, Tennessee. My two brothers are close by and check in with her on a regular basis. It often appears to us as if her world has shrunk to the edge of extinction—complicated by multiple physical infirmities, not the least of which is her loss of hearing.

I can't help but think, however, that the Lord comforts her in ways we cannot see, in a silent world with words we cannot hear, and with thoughts we cannot know. Sometimes it is in the silence that we hear the "still small voice" of the Lord most clearly. In the silence we are able to remember the good things, to feel His presence, and to increase our expectation of His second coming.

*Mary Fanneita Bomar Finley*
*my mother*

*He who dwells in the secret place of the Most High shall abide under the shadow of the Almighty.*
*I will say of the LORD, "He is my refuge and my fortress; my God, in Him I will trust."*

*Surely He shall deliver you from the snare of the fowler and from the perilous pestilence.*
*He shall cover you with His feathers, and under His wings you shall take refuge; His truth shall be your shield and buckler. You shall not be afraid of the terror by night, nor of the arrow that flies by day, nor of the pestilence that walks in darkness, nor of the destruction that lays waste at noonday.*

*A thousand may fall at your side, And ten thousand at your right hand; but it shall not come near you. Only with your eyes shall you look, And see the reward of the wicked.*

*Because you have made the LORD, who is my refuge, even the Most High, your dwelling place, no evil shall befall you, nor shall any plague come near your dwelling; for He shall give His angels charge over you, to keep you in all your ways. In their hands they shall bear you up, lest you dash your foot against a stone. You shall tread upon the lion and the cobra, the young lion and the serpent you shall trample underfoot.*

*"Because he has set his love upon Me, therefore I will deliver him; I will set him on high, because he has known My name. He shall call upon Me, and I will answer him; I will be with him in trouble; I will deliver him and honor him. With long life I will satisfy him, And show him My salvation."*
Psalm 90(91)

It's hard for me to write about my mother; words seem insufficient to express the proper gratitude for her life of sacrifice in total service to others. On the occasion of my dad's retirement from his pastorate at Trinity Baptist Church, I did write these words to her:

*March 21, 1989*

*Dear Mother,*

*On the occasion of Daddy's retirement as the pastor of Trinity Baptist Church, I would like to also recognize your 38 years of ministry at the Church. Your faithfulness to Daddy and to the Church through the years has not gone unnoticed by God and by others, especially your sons.*

*Your love and respect for Daddy through the years enabled him to successfully pastor the Church. A pastor's wife can make or break his ministry, and you made it. For that reason, all of Daddy's accomplishments are also yours.*

*You have sacrificed so many things in life to insure that the Lord's work would continue and prosper. You raised a family of five in a two-bedroom house. You gave of your time in so many ways to serve the Church as a musician and as an educator. Unlike some women who took their degrees[79] and sought careers for their own glory and prestige, you used the knowledge that God gave you and shared it with others that they might grow up to love and serve the living God.*

*But more than all these things, I love you just because you're my mother. You gave birth to me and comforted and protected me. When I was hungry you fed me. You clothed me and took care of me when I was sick. You taught me to obey. You taught me to respect my father. You taught me to love God. You taught me to sing. You prayed for my salvation and you took me to Church.*

*You loved me even when I was disobedient, when I was disrespectful and unloving, when I did not help and did not care, just because you are my mother and because a mother's love is inexhaustible.*

*You helped me to find my heart, to find God's will for my life, to find my place in the Church and in society.*

*Perhaps the most characteristic thing about God's love is self-sacrifice. And when I look at your life, Mother, I see God and His love for others.*

*May He richly bless you in these days and may God grant you many years!*

*Your son,*
*John David*

---

[79] She earned a Master's degree in Religious Education from Southern Baptist Theological Seminary in Lousivill, Kentucky in 1951.

CHAPTER 8 ~ *Viva la Fiesta!*

Needless to say, the Spanish Colonial influence has left a permanent mark on the culture of Southern California. Each year during the late summer, Old Spanish Days are celebrated in Santa Barbara with traditional costumes, dancing, arts, crafts and, of course, food.

Over the years, we have developed quite a taste for Mexican Food, but I have begun to discover more recently some significant differences in a more authentic Mexican cuisine and Tex-Mex or Southwestern style.

The taco is a classic example: You don't buy taco shells in the store, you deep fat fry your own. You don't use ground beef; you use shredded beef or chicken. Cumin is more prominent than chili powder and cabbage preferred over lettuce. You don't use salsa from a jar or can, you dice your own tomatoes, add a bunch of chopped cilantro, diced onions and finely diced fresh jalapeño or pasilla chili peppers and call it Pico de Gallo. Fresh jalapeños are much preferred over pickled jalapeño slices, and Queso Ranchero over grated Cheddar or Monterey Jack cheese.

## Any Old Cheese Won't Do

Cheese in Mexico is produced on ranches concentrated in areas like Chihuahua, Oaxaca, Querétaro and Chiapas. Here are some of the most common types of Mexican cheeses that you'll find in the dairy section of our local supermarket chains:

QUESO FRESCO: (also known as Queso Ranchero) is a soft, mild, white cheese that can be easily crumbled by hand. This slightly salty cheese is the most popular style among Hispanics. It is used for chile rellenos, enchiladas and tostadas, or grated over your favorite Mexican foods. It can also be served alone as a breakfast side, as a snack or as an appetizer.

Originally developed in Burgos, Spain, this cheese is made with a combination of cow and goat milk and can be used in any dish calling for ricotta, cottage cheese or feta. It can also be used as a substitute for mozzarella in Italian salads.

If you can find genuine queso fresco in bulk (not prepackaged or processed), that's the best. Look for the El Mexicano brand.

QUESO PANELA: A mild, natural curd cheese with a very soft, creamy texture. It is served cubed with fruit, in salads and soups or sliced in sandwiches.

QUESO OAXACA: The best cheese for melting, it's a stretched curd cheese wound into balls. You pull thin strings off to fill tortillas or make nachos or quesadillas.

QUESO ENCHILADO: A hard, aged cheese similar to Romano. It is coated with a mild chili paste to add some spice. It can be used to stuff enchiladas or grate over Mexican dishes.

QUESO COTIJA: A cheese made with whole milk and then aged. It is dry and salty with a sharp flavor much like Parmesan. It is used as a condiment, grated over food or salads.

QUESO REQUESÓN: Ricotta-like cheese good for making spreads or filling enchiladas.

QUESO MANCHEGO: From the Spanish region of La Mancha, this is a buttery yellow cheese good for serving with fruit and bread.

## PICO DE GALLO

1 large onion, diced
1 bunch cilantro, stemmed and finely chopped
1 fresh jalapeño, seeded and diced
1tsp cumin (use more if you like)
1 lime, juiced
garlic salt to taste
2-3 tomatoes, diced

Mix diced onion and finely chopped cilantro together in a medium mixing bowl. Add seeded and diced jalapeño, cumin, lime juice, garlic salt and mix again. Finally, add diced tomatoes and stir gently.

*Note: When I dice tomatoes, I use a fillet knife. The extra sharp tip and thin blade work well to finely dice the tomatoes without turning them into mush.*

## CHIPOTLE SALSA
1 batch of Pico de Gallo
7oz can Chipotle Peppers in Adobo Sauce
2-8oz cans tomato sauce
1-2c water

Make a batch of Pico de Gallo and place in a medium mixing bowl. Add tomato sauce, 1 cup of water and stir. Puree a can of Chipotle Peppers in a food processor. Add one tablespoon at a time to the mixture, stir and taste for desired heat factor. This is powerful stuff! Use the second cup of water if you get it too hot or if you like a thinner consistency for your salsa. Serve with tortilla chips and Mexican Cervesa[80] (lager beer) or Horchata[81].

## GUACAMOLE
2 avocados, sliced, pitted and spooned from peels
1 lime, juiced
2Tbl sour cream
1tsp picante sauce
garlic salt to taste
water to thin paste (optional)
1/2c Pico de Gallo (optional)

Slice avocados, remove large pits and remove light green flesh from peels with a large spoon. Place in a medium mixing bowl and mash with a potato masher. Add lime juice, sour cream and picante sauce and stir. Thin with water if a lighter consistency is desired. Add garlic salt to taste and Pico de Gallo if desired. Serve with chips and offer as a topping for tacos or enchiladas.

## TORTILLA CHIPS

If you've never made homemade chips you should try it. I like to take a fresh corn tortilla, slice it in half, stack the halves and slice them three ways to produce six wedges. Actually I stack two and get twelve wedges. Drop wedges into a deep-fat fryer at about 350F for about a minute.

---

[80] Lager style beers are actually much better with hot and spicy foods than ales, porters and stouts.
[81] Horchata is another drink that will put the fire out on spicy foods. It's made from rice flour, water, lime, sugar and cinnamon. I would suggest buying it in a prepackaged dry mix form and follow the package directions.

I use vegetable shortening. Remove, drain on paper towels and sprinkle with Lawry's Seasoned Salt.[82]

### BLACK BEAN SALSA
1 batch of Pico de Gallo
3-15oz cans black beans, drained

Make a batch of Pico de Gallo and place in a medium mixing bowl. Drain black beans in a colander. Add to Pico de Gallo and mix thoroughly.

### MEXICAN SLAW
1 head cabbage, finely chopped or shredded
1 bunch radishes, diced
3 green onions, finely chopped
2Tbl sugar
3Tbl fresh lime juice
a dash of cumin powder
garlic salt to taste

Combine cabbage, radishes and green onions in a large mixing bowl. Combine sugar and lime juice. Pour over ingredients, add cumin, garlic salt and stir. Toss thoroughly, then let it sit for at least an hour. Toss occasionally. Serve as a side dish or as an appetizer with tortilla chips.

### CHEESE ENCHILADAS
vegetable shortening for frying
19oz can mild enchilada sauce
14.5oz can chicken broth
16oz requesón cheese, grated
1/2 onion, diced
12 corn tortillas
1Tbl cornstarch
2-3Tbl milk (or crème fresca)

In a cast iron pot (or electric deep-fat fryer) heat up vegetable shortening to 350F. In a medium mixing bowl combine enchilada sauce with chicken broth. In a second medium mixing bowl, combine cheese and diced onions.

---

[82] I know Lawry's is not very authentic, but when you try it, you'll thank me.

When oil has reached 350F, drop one tortilla at a time into the hot oil for 10 seconds. Lift from oil with tongs and drain. Drop into enchilada sauce mixture and coat, then transfer to 9x13 baking dish. Add about 2T of the cheese and onion mixture to each tortilla and fold up the sides. The second side should overlap the first side. The ends are left open. Line them up side-by-side in the baking dish.

In a small cup add 1T cornstarch and 2-3T milk. Mix thoroughly until cornstarch is dissolved. In a 1qt saucepan, combine remaining enchilada sauce with cornstarch mixture over medium heat. Stir with a whisk until thickened, then cover and remove from heat. Pour thickened enchilada sauce over enchiladas and sprinkle any remaining cheese and onion mixture on top. Makes 12 enchiladas.

## CRAB ENCHILADA CASSEROLE

vegetable shortening
19fl oz mild enchilada sauce (go with medium if you like heat)
14.5oz chicken broth
15oz cream style corn
8oz cream cheese[83]
3.8oz black olives, sliced
4oz green chilies, diced
1 large onion, diced
1 bunch cilantro, thoroughly rinsed and diced
1lb imitation crabmeat, chopped (unless, of course, you can find the real thing)
cumin and garlic powder to taste (use a lot!)
1pkg corn tortillas (at least 18 tortillas)

In a cast iron pot (or electric deep-fat fryer) heat vegetable shortening to 350F. In a medium mixing bowl combine enchilada sauce with chicken broth. In a second medium mixing bowl, combine cream style corn with cream cheese. Add olives, chilies, diced onion and cilantro to mixture and stir. Finally, chop imitation crab and add to mixture. Add cumin and garlic powder to taste and mix thoroughly.

When oil has reached 350F, drop one tortilla at a time into the hot oil for 10 seconds. Lift from oil with tongs and drain over the oil. Drop into enchilada sauce mixture and coat, then transfer to 9x13 baking dish and begin lining the bottom of the dish. Line the bottom with 6 tortillas.

Cover with 1/2 of the crab mixture then add a second layer of tortillas. Finally, add the rest of the crab mixture and add a layer of tortillas on top. Spoon some of the remaining enchi-

[83] During the Lenten Season and fast days, I use a non-dairy substitute: Tofutti (imitation cream cheese) or IMO (imitation sour cream). At the same time I substitute vegetable broth or water for the chicken broth.

lada sauce over the tortillas on top to keep them moist. Cover with foil and bake at 350F for 30 minutes. Let cool for 10 minutes before serving.

## WINE MARGARITAS (BLENDED)
12fl oz frozen limeade
750ml bottle of white wine
crushed ice
2 limes, sliced
salt

In a blender combine frozen limeade and wine. Blend on a low speed for 10-15 seconds. Pour 2-1/4 cups liquid into a separate container leaving 2-1/4 cups in the blender. Pack with crushed ice until the liquid reaches the 5-cup level. Blend on high speed until thoroughly mixed and an icy mixture forms.

Prepare the rims of the margarita glasses by rubbing a little lime juice on them then dipping them into salt. Shake off excess salt, add the blended margarita mixture, top with slices of lime and you're in business. Repeat process with reserved mixture. Makes 10-12 servings.


## FISH TACOS

I particularly like to make fish tacos from smaller fillets like perch or ocean rockfish. Rub or spray small fillets with oil and sprinkle heavily with a Cajun-style or some other spicy rub. I like to mix equal parts salt, pepper, garlic powder, chili powder and paprika; then add a little cayenne for an extra kick.

Fry in a hot cast iron skillet for just a couple of minutes on each side. Break into small chunks with a spatula as the fish begins to flake.

Spoon onto warm corn tortillas and stuff with shredded cabbage (or lettuce). Top with salsa verde (green) and sour cream. Tapatio (salsa picante) is great too, if salsa verde is not your favorite.

If you are using larger fillets, you can cut them into strips about the size of your index finger and deep-fry the fish according to the recipe[84] instructions. See Index.

---

[84] During the Lenten season, I simply roll the filleted fish strips in a dry mixture of flour and cornmeal in equal parts, drop them into the oil or if I can find a boxed dry mixture for fish, I use that. Place fried fillets on warm corn tortillas and add ingredients listed above.

## SALSA VERDE

1lb tomatillos (green tomato-like vegetables), husked and rinsed
2c water (or 14.5oz can chicken broth)
1 bunch green onions, chopped
3 large garlic cloves
2 Serrano chilies, seeded and diced
1 bunch fresh cilantro leaves
1 fresh lime, juiced
Adobo[85] to taste

Place tomatillos in water (or chicken broth) and bring to a boil. Reduce heat, cover and simmer for about 5 minutes or until tomatillos are soft. Combine remaining ingredients in a medium mixing bowl. Transfer tomatillos to blender with a slotted spoon and puree. Add remaining ingredients to blender and puree until smooth. Add more Adobo to taste. Transfer to a serving bowl (chill if desired). Makes about 3-1/2 cups. Save chicken broth for soup. This sauce is also fantastic over broiled salmon or scrambled eggs. Warm before serving.

## CHILI VERDE SOUP

*Sometimes I double this recipe*
3c chicken broth
2lb boneless pork top loin or pork butt[86], trimmed of fat
1tsp Mexican oregano
1 recipe of Salsa Verde (using chicken broth)
2 medium potatoes, chopped

Add chicken broth to a Dutch oven. Divide pork roast into three or four large chunks, trim the fat and add to broth. Add oregano and simmer until pork is tender. Remove meat to cool. In the meantime prepare Salsa Verde according to recipe instructions (using chicken broth). After removing meat, add potatoes and simmer until potatoes are soft. Add Salsa Verde to soup pot. Finally, chop pork into small chunks and add it back into the soup. Serve with hot buttered cornbread. Serves 4.

---

[85] Adobo is an all-purpose seasoning made of salt, garlic powder, oregano and turmeric.
[86] You'll probably only be able to find a 3.5-4lb roast. Use half of the meat for the soup and reserve the other half for something else (like a sandwich the next day).

## FISH FILLETS SIMMERED IN SALSA

This is really so easy. Just use a large skillet with a lid. Lightly spray the skillet with canola oil, add fish fillets and smother in salsa. Place the lid on the skillet, reduce the heat and simmer for 20 minutes. Serve with Spanish rice.

### SPANISH RICE
2Tbl corn oil
1-1/4c rice
2c chicken broth
1/2c tomato sauce
1/2tsp salt
1/4tsp chili powder to taste (optional)

Heat oil in a skillet. Add rice and stir constantly over medium heat until browned. Add chicken broth, tomato sauce and salt. Stir for a minute or two. Add a touch of chili powder if you like. Bring to a boil. Reduce heat and simmer uncovered for about 15-20 minutes.

### CEVICHE
2c fresh squeezed lime juice
2lb very fresh fish, diced (corbina, pompano or red snapper)
3-4 bay leaves
one batch Pico de Gallo
more salt and cumin to taste

First, prepare 2c fresh squeezed lime juice and add to a large mixing bowl. Dice fresh fish into 1/4" cubes and add to lime juice along with 3 or 4 bay leaves. Set aside to marinate for at least 3-4 hours. It's best to refrigerate overnight. Stir occasionally.

Prepare a batch of Pico de Gallo. When fish has marinated in the lime juice and bay leaves a sufficient amount of time to turn white and begin to flake, drain and add to the batch of Pico de Gallo. Remove bay leaves, mix thoroughly then add more salt and cumin to taste. Cumin is an essential ingredient, so don't be bashful. Serve on corn tostada shells.

# Albondigas (Meatball Soup)

## Meatballs
1/2lb lean ground beef
1/2lb lean ground pork
1 medium onion, minced
1Tbl fresh mint, minced (or 1tsp dried)
1 egg, slightly beaten
1/2tsp salt
cumin to taste
3Tbl uncooked rice

## Broth
6c chicken stock
1 bunch green onions, finely chopped
2 garlic cloves, minced
2 carrots, sliced
1 zucchini, chopped
2 potatoes, cubed
16oz can diced tomatoes
salt to taste

Place all the ingredients for the meatballs in a bowl, mix together thoroughly. Form small meatballs. Moisten your hands frequently with cold water to prevent the meat from sticking. I like to use a large melon baller to form the meatballs.

In a large pot or Dutch oven, add the chicken stock and bring to a boil. Slowly add the meatballs and return to a second boil; skim if necessary. Reduce heat; add onions, garlic and diced tomatoes with their juice. Cover and simmer 20 minutes. Add carrots, zucchini and potatoes. Check for seasoning and salt if necessary. Cover and continue cooking for 30 minutes.

Garnish with fresh salsa, sour cream, chopped cilantro, fried tortilla strips and avocado cubes.

## PAN DE MUERTE[87]

1 package dry yeast (or 2-1/4 tsp from a jar)
1/2c lukewarm water (105F)
5-6c flour (plus additional flour for kneading)
1tsp salt
3/4c sugar
1c butter, melted and cooled
6 eggs, lightly beaten
2Tbl anise water[88] (or 1tsp anise extract)
2Tbl orange blossom water (or the grated rind of one whole orange)

### ICING

1-1/2c confectioner's sugar
1tsp vanilla
milk (about 1/4c)
pink sugar crystals

Dissolve yeast in water and add 1 cup of flour. Stir to make a soft sponge, cover with a cloth and let rise in a warm place until doubled in bulk.

To the yeast mixture, add the rest of the flour mixed with salt and sugar, and the cooled butter that has been mixed with eggs, anise and orange blossom water or grated rind. Mix well and turn out onto a floured board. Dough will be soft so keep hands floured and knead lightly. Place into a bowl and set in a warm place for about 1to1-1/2 hours to rise. Dough should double in volume.

Shape into a round loaf (it helps to have a round baking pan for support). Traditionally, about 1/4 of the dough is used to decorate the top of each loaf with a skull and crossbones. These shapes are attached just before baking.

Divide the dough to be used for decoration into three parts. Roll one part into a smooth ball. Roll the other two into strips a little shorter than the diameter of the loaf, and form knobs (that look like bones) at either end. Place the strips across the main part of the bread forming crossbones and place the round ball of dough in the middle to form the "skull." Press your finger deeply into the ball to form the eye sockets in the skull.

Bake in a preheated 350F oven for about 50 minutes. Cool and frost with confectioner's sugar mixed with vanilla and only enough milk to make a glaze of frosting consistency (only the top is frosted). Sprinkle with pink sugar crystals. Makes one loaf.

---

[87] On the Orthodox Christian Calendar we celebrate All Saints Day on the Sunday after Pentecost. On the Roman calendar, however, All Saint's Day is November 1st.
[88] To make anise water put 1T anise seeds in 1/4c water and simmer for 3-4 minutes and then strain off seeds.

CHAPTER 9 ~ *He Sends the Springs into the Valleys...*

When I was in high school I spent my summers working at Church Camp. Actually, there were two: Camp Hudgens, located just a few miles north of McAlester on Lake McAlester; and Falls Creek Baptist Assembly, just outside Davis in Southern Oklahoma.

Falls Creek wasn't that far from Ardmore, and so on the weekends, I would drive down, or catch a ride down to Ardmore to stay with Grandma and Grandpa Bomar. As I'd pull into the driveway, often I would find my grandmother out on the front porch watering her ferns and African violets. She loved to make things grow.

During the summertime, their garden out in the back yard would flourish. It was a rather small plot, right behind the detached garage, but it was prolific: corn, green beans, potatoes, onions, green onions, carrots, squash, tomatoes; you name it, they grew it.

It seems so curious to me, as I think back on this: she had a large grapevine right in the middle of the back yard and a big fig tree at the side of the house. That fig tree was big enough for a boy to climb and get a stomachache full of figs when they were in season. They were smaller figs than I usually see out here in California. I don't know if the variety or the climate made them smaller, but they were still good. She would serve them fresh and then make some homemade fig preserves with what we couldn't consume on the spot. Preserves are really pretty simple to fix:

## FIG PRESERVES

*This same formula works for peaches, plums, apricots and probably just about any other soft fruit you would want to try.*

Combine equal parts of fresh figs and sugar and the juice of one lemon. Cook at low heat until juice turns to syrup and begins to thicken. It's that simple, but here are a few hints:

Chop fresh fruit about as small as you can without turning them to mush (they will turn to mush soon enough). Use a Dutch oven, but do not cover with a lid. Add fruit first and then sugar. Use low heat so as not to burn either the fruit or the sugar. As the fruit and sugar begin to dissolve, stir slowly and mix thoroughly. Check and stir often. The preserves should develop a very slow boil. It looks kind of like a smoldering volcano.

You never can tell how long it's going to take, but there is one caution: When the preserves cool, they will thicken significantly. So, stop before the syrup gets too thick. Think about this: how does warm maple syrup or honey pour vs. refrigerated maple syrup or honey? Quite a bit faster, right? I would go for the consistency of room-temperature "real" maple syrup, then turn it off.

Remember, canning should only be done with the proper equipment, clear and reliable instructions and a very clean environment.[89]

## Summertime... and the Livin' was Easy

Anyway, I would usually arrive from a hot week of summer camp in the Arbuckle Mountains on Saturday around noontime. Bomie[90] would sit me down at the dining room table and serve up a huge glass of sweetened iced tea, a plate full of pressure-cooked vegetables from the garden, fresh corn carved from the cob and some hot buttered cornbread.

My favorite was a combination of pressure-cooked green beans, carrots, small red new potatoes and pearl onions, all right out of their garden. Her secret was to sprinkle a little sugar on them before closing the lid.

### PRESSURE-COOKED SUMMER VEGETABLES
8-10 new potatoes, halved or quartered
4-5 small to medium sized carrots
1 fist full (or more) pearl onions, peeled
1lb fresh green beans, cut
salt, pepper and sugar to taste

You can use regular red potatoes if you can't find any new potatoes. Just pick the smallest you can find and quarter them. Small carrots are great whole, but larger carrots should be cut in half and the thick end should be halved lengthwise. Pearl onions may be hard to find. If so, just use regular white or yellow onions and quarter them. There is no substitute for fresh green beans. Cut the stems and depending on size, you can leave the small ones whole, cut the medium-sized in half and the large ones in thirds.

---

[89] Check out www.homecanning.com for proper canning procedures.
[90] Our nickname for Grandma Bomar.

If you have a pressure cooker, it's really pretty simple. Just add a little water, place the steamer grate in the bottom of the cooker. Add potatoes, carrots, onions. Sprinkle with salt and pepper. Add fresh cut green beans last, sprinkling with a little more salt and pepper and if you like, a little sugar. Steam under full pressure for about 4 minutes. If you don't have a pressure cooker you can do this in a Dutch oven with a steamer tray and lid, but it's going to take about an hour on low heat for the vegetables to soften.

## ICED TEA

It may seem silly to give an iced tea recipe—you know: Boil water. Insert tea bags. Steep. Get a big tall glass. Add ice. Pour tea into glass. Add lemon wedge, sugar and stir. Drink.

Actually, Sun Tea is really nice and many people don't know that you can make tea without boiling water. Get a clear (preferably glass) gallon container. Add about 12 tea bags. Cover with clear plastic wrap and set out in the sun for several hours. Add 1/8tsp baking soda, 1c sugar and 2 lemons thinly sliced and stir. The nice thing about sun tea is that it doesn't cloud up after refrigeration. Enjoy.

Other foods remind me so much of my grandmother: bread and butter pickles, a sliced red-ripe tomato, fried okra, or a steamed summer crook-necked squash, sliced, buttered and salted. She also loved to make sandwiches with pimiento cheese.

### FRIED OKRA
vegetable shortening
1lb fresh okra
2 eggs, beaten
1/2c buttermilk
1c flour
1c cornmeal
1Tbl baking powder
1tsp salt
1/4tsp black pepper

Heat vegetable shortening in a deep-fat fryer and heat to 350-375F. In the meantime, wash okra and slice into 1/2 inch slices; pat dry with paper towels. Combine eggs and buttermilk; add okra, and let stand for 10 minutes. Combine flour, cornmeal, baking powder, salt and pepper. Drain okra using a slotted spoon, and dredge a few slices at a time in the flour mixture. Fry until golden brown. Drain on paper towels and serve immediately. Don't forget the ketchup. Makes 4 servings.

## PIMIENTO CHEESE SANDWICH SPREAD

1lb American cheese[91], grated (no substitutes)
4oz jar pimientos with liquid, diced
1/2c mayonnaise
2tsp sugar (or 1Tbl sweet pickle juice)
1/4tsp cayenne pepper (optional)
1/2 onion, minced (optional)

Grate cheese and set aside. In a food processor add liquid from pimiento jar, mayonnaise, sugar (or sweet pickle juice) and cayenne pepper and blend. Slowly add a about 1/2c grated cheese to mayonnaise mixture until spread begins to thicken. Transfer to mixing bowl, add diced pimientos, onions and remaining grated cheese. Mix ingredients together and allow them to mellow in the refrigerator overnight. Spread on crackers or use for sandwich filling.

## *That Garden of Eden*

I don't always succeed in planting a vegetable garden each spring, but when I do I think of my grandmother. When I turn the dirt with a shovel, get down on my hands and knees, and break up the clods of dirt in my hands, I think of her. I think of some of her favorite hymns I sang with her in church:

Have Thine own way, Lord! Have Thine own way!
Thou art the potter, I am the clay;
Mold me and make me After Thy will,
While I am waiting, Yielded and still.

"Yet, O Lord, you are our Father; we are the clay, and you are the potter; we are all the work of your hand." Isaiah 64:8

There is something both humbling and healing to the soul when we assume the posture of bended knees. The hardness of our hearts is broken, the seeds are sown in the good soil, the waters of salvation cover us and our lives sprout, bringing forth new life and good fruit. Living in the city, how often do we lose this connection with the earth from which we came? How difficult it is for us to understand the imagery and spiritual lessons contained in the Holy Scriptures. Yet when we taste the fruit from the vine, whether it be tomatoes, squash or whatever, and we planted, watered and nurtured it to maturity...how sweet it is!

---

[91] Processed cheese and processed cheese food are not the same. Do not use cheese food.

I can taste it now! Really what I taste is Bomie's love, her concern for me and for my future. I remember one moment in my life, a pivotal moment in my relationship with God, which occurred after one of her meals. My mother had told Bomie that I was beginning to compose music and so she wanted to hear what I was doing. "Come over here to the organ and play me some of your new songs."

She knew I was really caught up in my trumpet playing and loved being in the high school band. She knew I had placed third in a recent state trumpet competition in Stillwater. She knew I had been talking about majoring in music at Oklahoma State, Oklahoma University or North Texas State, toward pursuing a career as a band director.

She also knew that the music I was composing was for the Church and she wanted to reinforce that direction. With all the love she could muster, but with a firm conviction and direction she said to me, "John, it is so obvious to me that God gave you a talent in music, and I want you to promise me you will use that talent to glorify God." I promised her I would, and that promise has remained with me throughout my life. I love music, all kinds, but the music of the Church remains number one.

In the quiet of my heart, I often return to that Garden of Eden, that paradise of the Kingdom, where God once promised, that "every man shall sit under his vine and under his fig tree, and none shall make them afraid."[92] As I taste the heavenly bread and the cup of life, I give thanks to God for that person who cared enough and dared enough to challenge me in my dedication to the things above, and watered me with her love and desire to see me grow into the person God wants me to be.

*Anabel Tyson Bomar*
*my maternal grandmother*
*b. June 6, 1889 d. Jan. 17, 1981*

*The Lord is my shepherd; I shall not want. He maketh me to lie down in green pastures; he leadeth me beside the still waters. He restoreth my soul: he leadeth me in the paths of righteousness for his name's sake.*

*Yea, though I walk through the valley of the shadow of death, I will fear no evil: for thou art with me; thy rod and thy staff they comfort me.*

*Thou preparest a table before me in the presence of mine enemies; thou anointest my head with oil; my cup runneth over. Surely goodness and mercy shall follow me all the days of my life; and I will dwell in the house of the Lord forever.*[93] Psalm 22(23)

*"Let the words of my mouth and*
*the meditation of my heart be*
*acceptable in Thy sight, O Lord my*
*Rock and My Redeemer."* Psalm 19:14

[92] Micah 4:4
[93] My Grandmother was often quoted as saying "Faith is taking God at His Word." Perhaps this is why she so loved the 23rd Psalm.

## CHAPTER 10 ~ *Wine That Makes Glad the Heart of Man*

*Bless, O Lord, this new fruit of the vine, which thou hast graciously been pleased to permit to come to maturity, through calm seasons and gentle rains and favorable weather; and let it be unto joy for those of us who shall partake of this offspring of the vine; and may we offer it as a gift to thee unto the purification of our sins, through the sacred and holy Body and Blood of thy Christ, with whom thou art blessed together with thine all-holy and good and life-giving Spirit, now and ever, and unto ages of ages. Amen.[94]*

The evening service of Vespers begins with Psalm 103 (104), that great Psalm recalling the goodness of Creation:

*Bless the Lord, O my soul. O Lord my God, Thou art very great...*

*...He sends springs into the valleys...that he may bring forth food out of the earth: And wine that makes glad the heart of man, and oil to make his face to shine, and bread which strengthens man's heart...*

*O Lord, how manifold are Thy works! In wisdom hast Thou made them all:*

[94] Prayer for Blessing Grapes on the Feast of the Transfiguration (August 6)

Wine, oil, bread: these elements presented by mankind to God in the Church express our interaction with the creation. God makes grapes, but we care for them and we make wine. God makes olives, but we extract the oil. God makes wheat; we make bread. We offer these things to God with the expectation that he will transform them and give them back to us as the means by which we enter into and sustain a living communion with Him, our fellow man and the whole cosmos. In this great dialogue and movement of gratitude and love, it is possible for our hearts to be truly strengthened and made glad and for our faces to shine with the radiance of His Glory.

Father Alexander Schmemann begins his book, *For the Life of the World*, with these words:

> *"Man is what he eats." Man must eat in order to live; he must take the world into his body and transform it into himself, into flesh and blood. He is indeed that which he eats, and the whole world is presented as one all-embracing banquet table for man. And this image of the banquet remains, throughout the whole Bible, the central image of life. It is the image of life at its creation and also the image of life at its end and fulfillment: "...that you eat and drink at my table in my Kingdom."* [95]

In her book, *Great Wine Made Simple*, Andrea Immer states, "despite extensive ongoing research, relatively little is known about how fermentation's chemical reactions result in complex scents in wine, and thus very little is in the winemaker's control."[96] How true, and how even more amazing that our loving God, Who created not only the mystery of complex scents resulting from fermentation, but also transforms wine into His Life-giving Blood (which is very little in the priest's control), would present this gift of salvation to us in the Eucharist[97] of the Church.

Wine is medicine. Wine is an expression of love. Wine is communion. Wine is a mystery. Wine drinking, in moderation of course, can be a celebration of joy. Aren't many doctors now saying that a glass of red wine at dinner is good for the heart? I wonder where they got such an idea?[98]

In these pages, I would like to offer a few fundamentals for understanding and enjoying the mystery of wine. But how can we understand the mystery? Let us "taste and see."

---

[95] Alexander Schmemann, *For the Life of the World* (Crestwood, N.Y.: St. Vladimir's Seminary Press, 1973), p. 11.
[96] Andrea Immer, *Great Wine Made Simple*, (New York: Broadway Books, 2002), p. 69.
[97] "Eucharist," which means "thanksgiving," refers to the Liturgy of the Church.
[98] Psalm 103 (104): 15

## Body Styles of Wine

Among most wines that we commonly purchase, there are three basic body styles: light-bodied, medium-bodied and full-bodied. Several factors may give us clues about the body style of a particular wine before we even taste it: variety of grape, color of the wine and alcohol content. Often we don't even need a clue since the wine label itself may tell us if the wine is light, medium, or full-bodied.

A light-bodied premium white wine, like a Riesling, will have a pale yellow-green color, and an alcohol content of about 12-13%. A light-bodied premium red, like a Pinot Noir, will have a dark pink color, and an alcohol content of about 12.5-13.5%.

A medium-bodied premium white wine, like a Sauvignon Blanc, will have a straw yellow color, and an alcohol content of 13-14%. A medium-bodied premium red wine, like a merlot, will have a ruby red color, and about the same alcohol range.

A full-bodied premium white wine, like a Chardonnay, will have a yellow-gold color, and an alcohol content of about 13.5-14.5%. A full-bodied red, like a cabernet sauvignon, will have an inky, dark purple color, and the higher alcohol range as found in the full-bodied white.

## Learning How to Taste

About wine tasting Andrea says, "It isn't just about what you feel on your tongue. Wine stirs all of your senses: seeing, smelling, touching, tasting—and even hearing—as you clink glasses for the toast."[99] So let's go through this sensory experience step by step. First, we need to discuss:

### WINE GLASSES

"The choice of glassware will influence the sight, aroma and taste of a wine."[100] Clear glass and thin-rimmed bowls are signs of quality glassware for wine. Generally speaking, the stem of the glass should be about as long as the bowl is tall.

"A large bowl and a narrow opening work together to magnify the wine's bouquet. They give plenty of space for the aromas to expand, but only a narrow escape."[101] White wine glasses tend to be on the smaller end of the spectrum with narrower openings and the red wine glasses are usually larger with wider openings.[102]

---

[99] Ibid, p. 7.
[100] Bruce Sanderson, "Storing and Serving Wine" —Excerpted from Wine Spectator Magazine's (online) Guide to Great Wine Values.
[101] Ibid.
[102] I have observed the following from wine glasses purchased onsite for tasting at wineries: Most wine glasses range from 6-9" in height, have an opening of 1 3/4"-2 3/4", and hold from 8-12oz of wine. Since we don't want to fill a wine glass more than half full, a typical serving would be about 4-6oz.

## SEEING

For purposes of examining and tasting wine, fill a glass no more than one-third full. We don't hold the glass by the bowl, because (now think carefully...) that's right, you can't see the wine! Also fingerprints can blur the color of the wine, and heat from your hand can raise the wine's temperature.

Color gives us clues to several things: First the hue, best judged by tilting the glass and looking at the wine through the rim, may help us judge whether the wine is light, medium, or full-bodied. Second, the intensity, which may help us to recognize the variety of grape, is gauged by looking straight down through the wine from above. This is the way God looks at wine. As Thomas Matthews puts it, "No other liquid... reflects light with such joy and finesse."[103]

Finally, the clarity, whether the wine is brilliant or cloudy with particles, is most evident when light is shining sideways through the glass. Whether you are looking at a white or red wine, if it appears to be turning brown, there is a good chance the wine has oxidized, just like the flesh of an apple turns brown when it is cut and exposed to air. Oxidation in wine is usually caused by poor storage or a faulty cork seal that allowed air into the bottle, resulting in the loss of flavor and scent. Sometimes it turns to vinegar and tastes downright bad.

## SWIRLING AND SMELLING

Swirling the wine in your glass causes the alcohol to vaporize, carrying the scent of the wine to your nose. Obviously, the aroma and bouquet of the wine should be pleasant. After taking in a big whiff, you may be tempted to say, "Smells go-o-o-d!" Let me suggest saying, "Excellent bouquet!" If there's too much of an air of sophistication in that, then just say "Wow" or "Amazing." That will get you by.

It's interesting to think about the role of the nose in recognizing flavors. For instance, most people can smell the difference between bowls of vanilla and chocolate ice cream without seeing or tasting them. Since flavor is discerned by scent, we need to swirl in order to appreciate the true flavor of the wine.

In addition, swirling gives yet another clue as to the body style of the wine. Perhaps you've heard someone refer to "legs" when swirling a glass of wine. Legs are neither good nor bad, they simply reveal the fullness of the body and perhaps the amount of alcohol in the wine: generally speaking, the more alcohol, the more legs. So, a light-bodied wine, white or red, should have thin, fast-streaming legs (if any) running down the side of the glass after you swirl. A medium-bodied wine—a little thicker, a little slower and a full-bodied wine—thick, slow legs.

---

[103] Thomas Matthews, "The ABC's of Wine Tasting." http://www.winespectator.com/Wine/Wine_Basics/ (9/30/96)

## TASTING

Beyond the ability to distinguish tastes such as sweet, salty, sour and bitter, the tongue can also sense body and texture. By body, I mean the feeling of weight, richness and thickness of wine in the mouth, whereas texture might be likened to the sensation of bubbles in a sparkling wine. It's important to roll the wine around in your mouth, bringing it into contact with every part of your tongue. Learning to understand body is perhaps the most fundamental concept in the appreciation of wine. Comparison usually helps in learning new things, so let's try to understand "body" in terms of milk. Andrea gives the following description:

**Skim milk**—Watery, runny, feels kind of skimpy on your tongue
and the taste goes away fast—is light-bodied.
**Whole milk**—Thicker, richer, coats your mouth a bit,
and the flavor lingers longer—is medium bodied.
**Heavy cream**—Dense, thick, really clings to the inside of
your mouth, and the flavor hangs on—is full-bodied.[104]

## DRY, SWEET, BITTER, CRISP, OAKEY, TANNIC

"**Dry**" (a descriptive term often seen on wine labels) usually means there is a slightly higher alcohol content in the wine, since it is the grape's sugar that turns to alcohol in the fermentation process. When the fermentation process runs its normal course, most, if not all the sugar in the grape juice turns to alcohol, resulting in a "dry" taste. The heat of the alcohol is felt in the back of the throat.

"**Residual sugar**" means not all the sugar turned to alcohol during fermentation. Maybe the winemaker purposely stopped the fermentation process early in order to retain a bit of sweetness in the wine. Whichever the case, the sweetness is usually sensed on the top front area of the tongue.

"**Off-dry**" means "slightly sweet." So, why don't they just say slightly sweet? Because most wine snobs like only dry wine. They would drink something off dry, but never slightly sweet. It's kind of like the guy who would never buy a used car, but might consider a pre-owned vehicle.

"**Bitterness**," which is not a good thing, is more commonly found in reds and is sensed on the back of the tongue.

"**Crisp**," a word used to describe high acidity, that tart and tangy mouthwatering feeling, is felt on the sides of the tongue. Whites tend to be more "crisp" (acidic) than reds and Riesling and Sauvignon Blanc usually are more "crisp" than the softer, plumper and smoother taste of Chardonnay. Acid, here, is not a bad word. It's kind of like comparing a Granny Smith to a Fuji or Gala apple. My wife, a native of Washington State, loves the "crisp" taste of a Granny Smith.

"**Oakey**" is sometimes used to describe people like myself who are from Oklahoma (or is

---

[104] Andrea Immer, *Great Wine Made Simple* (New York: Broadway Books, 2002), pp. 15-16.

that "Okie"?), but in this case, "oakey" is the descriptive term for darker, more aromatic, richer tasting and fuller feeling wines that have been fermented and/or aged in oak barrels. This "oakey" taste is often described as toasty, smoky, sweet like vanilla (referring to a sweet-smelling scent, not sugar), or some combination of the three. Oak obviously adds complexity to the wine.

"**Tannic**" is that dried-out, leathery astringency of a red wine that make your cheeks pucker. If you've ever bitten into a persimmon, gotten a taste of banana peel, or chewed on the laces of your baseball glove, you know what I'm talking about.

In a wine context, tannin is a natural component of the skins, stems and seeds of wine grapes. That is why it is notable in red wines, not white—the juice, while soaking with the grape skins to get the red color, also soaks up the tannin.[105]

Low to medium tannin levels can feel silky and smooth, but high tannin levels, which often come from wine produced with "not fully ripened" grapes, can be harsh. Typically, Pinot Noir grapes, with their thinner grape skins, have lower tannin levels than the thicker-skinned Cabernet Sauvignon. As a general rule, we could say the darker the color of a red wine, the more tannin. Fortunately, the aging process can soften this effect over time and the tannin acts as a preservative during the wine's "time in a bottle."

## Aerating and Decanting

Another way to soften high tannin levels, especially in young wines, is to aerate them. Aerating involves pouring wine from a bottle into another container to let it "breathe." By doing so, the wine mixes with air and "opens up," giving it a better bouquet and smoother palate. A carafe works well for this purpose; you don't have to use a decanter.

Decanting is the process of separating wine from sediment in older red wines aged at least 10 years. When decanting an older wine, first stand the wine upright for 24-48 hours, so all the sediment (color and tannin molecules) sinks to the bottom of the bottle. Pour the wine into a decanter very carefully, leaving the last inch in the bottle.

## Storage

Since most wine is consumed within 24 to 48 hours of purchase, a small wine rack away from any direct heat source or sunlight will suffice for storage. If you plan to collect fine wines that benefit from additional aging, your basic requirements are darkness and steady temperature. Darkness is necessary because ultraviolet light can contribute to quicker wine spoilage. The steady temperature should be below 70F. Now you know the purpose of a wine cellar.

If you don't have a wine cellar, a basement can be a good spot (if it's not too damp), vacant space under a staircase, or on the floor in a downstairs closet. Avoid any place where the temperature could spike, causing the contents to expand, compromising the cork seal and resulting in a spoiled wine due to oxidation. Store your wines on their sides, either in cases or racked.

105 Ibid., p. 37.

## SERVING TEMPERATURES

Chill sparkling wines and light-bodied whites before serving, but don't use the refrigerator to store wine. Don't go too cold either, over chilling wines mutes their flavor. Fuller-bodied whites, such as Chardonnay, can be served slightly warmer.

You have probably heard that red wines should be served at room temperature, and you are right. However, the term "room temperature" refers to rooms in Europe way back when, and they were around 60F, not the 70-75 we find in most American homes. The slightly colder temperature slows the evaporation of alcohol, thus improving the aroma and flavor, and making the wine smoother. So, if you can figure out a way to bring a red down to about 62-65F before serving, try it. Careful though, the cooler the red gets, the more rough and bitter-tasting the tannins. Lighter reds like Pinot Noir can be served slightly cooler than full-bodied reds such as Cabernet Sauvignon and Syrah.

Here are some suggested serving temperatures for several popular white and red wines:

| | |
|---|---|
| Champagne: | 44-45F |
| Riesling, Sauvignon Blanc: | 50-55F |
| Chardonnay: | 55-60F |
| Pinot Noir: | 58-60F |
| Cabernet Sauvignon, Merlot: | 62-65F |

## MORE TASTING WORDS

**Grassy**–an aroma similar to fresh herbs, green vegetables or freshly cut grass usually found in Sauvignon Blanc.

**Buttery**–an aroma usually found in Chardonnay when malo-lactic fermentation creates a trace component called diacetyl, the same flavoring used in "butter"-flavored oil and movie theater popcorn.

**Spicy**–a sweet aroma similar to cinnamon, ginger, cloves, nutmeg or anise found in Gewurztraminer. Spicy can also describe the savory aroma of black pepper or cumin found in Syrah (Shiraz). You may also pick up some spicy sweet and black currant aromas in a Syrah.

**Floral**–an intoxicating perfume-like aroma similar to flower blossoms found in Muscat (Muscato).

**Fruity**–Well, since most wine is made from grapes, I hope it's fruity! But what do people mean when they describe a wine as "fruity?" Probably they are referring to the more "fruit-forward" style of American-made wines as opposed to the more "earthy" characteristics of their French counterparts.

Maybe "fruity" is a reference to characteristics that remind us of fruits other than, or in addition to a particular varietal grape, and it is common to describe their flavor in those terms. From a perspective of fruit types, one might describe a particular white wine's character as having hints or overtones of citrus, (like grapefruit, lemon or orange), apple, pear, pineapple, apricot, mango, etc. and a particular red's character in terms of cherry, plum, currant and various berry flavors.

## THE FINISH

After you swallow, exhale gently and slowly through both your nose and mouth. The retronasal passage, which connects the throat and the nose, is another avenue for aromas, which can linger long after the wine is finally swallowed. You'll find that the better the wine, the more complex, profound and long lasting these residual aromas can be. "With great wines, sensitive tasters and minimal distractions, the finish can last a minute or more. It's a moment of meditation and communion that no other beverage can create."[106]

## *Jesus' First Miracle*

> *On the third day there was a wedding in Cana of Galilee, and the mother of Jesus was there. Now both Jesus and His disciples were invited to the wedding. And when they ran out of wine, the mother of Jesus said to Him, "They have no wine." Jesus said to her, "Woman, what does your concern have to do with Me? My hour has not yet come."* John 2:1-4

At first glance, one might think that Jesus' attitude toward His Mother was less than respectful, but if we understand the Jewish idiom, which is hard to translate into English, we see exactly the opposite; that is, her elevation to one of dignity and equality. Woman (v.4) in ancient times was a title of respect and distinction. By addressing His Mother in this way, Jesus dignified womanhood.

*The Wedding of Cana*

"What does your concern have to do with me?" (v.4) might be translated literally: "What to me and to you?" or "What concern is that to me and to you?" Obviously Jesus is not refusing His Mother, neither is He putting her down; rather, He is elevating her to His own dignity.

As further proof of the honor and equality given by Christ to His Mother, in verse 5 she is now giving a command to the servants! In fact, Jesus' Mother gave the best advice ever

---

[106] Thomas Matthews, "The ABC's of Wine Tasting." http://www.winespectator.com/Wine/Wine_Basics/ (9/30/96)

given to mankind, when she spoke to the servants that day: "Whatever (Jesus) says to do, do it!" Obeying the will of God is the most important thing anyone can do.

Now there were set there six water pots of stone, according to the manner of purification of the Jews, containing twenty or thirty gallons apiece. Jesus said to them, "Fill the water pots with water." And they filled them up to the brim. And He said to them, "Draw some out now, and take it to the master of the feast."[107]

The disciples were given the privilege of beginning to see His Glory (v.11)[108], that is, the light, power and grace of God, and of beginning to have faith in Jesus as "God in the flesh."

So, why did Jesus turn the water into wine? He performed this miracle to show that the purifying element of the Old Testament, which was water, is now transformed in the New Testament into wine, that is, the Blood of Christ. The purifying element of the Old Covenant was water applied externally before one comes to the table, but the purifying element of the New Covenant is the blood of Christ, i.e., the wine of communion (the Eucharist) taken internally when one comes to the Lord's Table.[109] If Jesus could transform in a mystery, water into wine, then it helps me to believe He transforms (in a mystery) the bread and the wine into His Body and Blood.

## *The Mystery of Love*

It is important to remember that marriage as instituted by God existed in creation before the fall, before Christ became a man and outside the realm of the Church as such. It was instituted in Paradise and belongs to the very structure of human life. In other words, marriage as such, is not a uniquely Christian institution. Most ministers don't say anything fundamentally different than what a judge says in a civil marriage. "You will support the wife, she will support the husband, you will pledge a common life, you will educate your children, and you will have a common existence."

Rings also existed as a manifestation of marriage before Christ; the rings express eternity, faithfulness and something precious. When Pharaoh took off his ring and put it on Joseph's hand, he declared him to be equal in power in Egypt and they shared all things in common.[110] And when the Prodigal Son, who had turned from his sins, returned to his home seeking forgiveness, the Father ran out to meet him and kissed him, put a ring on his finger, forgave him and celebrated his return.[111] To hold all things in common and to maintain a spirit of forgiveness—this is the deeper meaning of the rings.

Unfortunately marriage, just like everything else, belongs to the fallen world. Marriage also has deteriorated through sin and just like fallen man, needs to be redeemed and transformed. So,

---

[107] John 2:6-8. By the way, assuming all the water in the pots turned to wine, this would equal between 53 and 80 cases.
[108] "This beginning of signs Jesus did in Cana of Galilee, and manifested His glory; and His disciples believed in Him." John 2:11
[109] The Orthodox Study Bible (Nashville, TN.: Thomas Nelson Publishers, 1993), p.215.
[110] Gen. 41:42
[111] Luke 15:22

in our Church, when the exchange of rings and the betrothal, i.e. the civil part of the marriage, is completed, the priest takes the couple and leads them in a procession to the front of the Church just below the Altar. This is extremely important because the procession reveals the transformation of marriage from being something merely natural, into marriage in Christ.

> *Marriage acquires here a new significance, a new dimension.*
> *This new "dimension" is Christ. He becomes the center of that*
> *relationship. Through Him marriage acquires an eternal significance,*
> *becomes a way to Christian fulfillment in the Kingdom of God.*[112]

And so, marriage does not last "until death us do part." We don't say that in our service, because marriage is supposed to last until "death to sin" unites us completely and unselfishly, in the same way that Christ died for us. I believe that the uncreated life of God, His glory, honor, light, power and grace are imparted to a newly married couple in the Sacrament (Mystery) of Holy Matrimony. Yes, in the ceremony itself. One might ask how this takes place; how does God do it? We don't know—that's why the Bible calls it a mystery! "This is a great mystery, but I speak concerning Christ and the Church."[113]

"O Lord our God, crown them with glory and honor." Through this request offered by the priest when the crowns are placed on the heads of the newly married couple,[114] God establishes a new family in Christ, a little Church, a little Kingdom in which the husband is "King" and his wife, "Queen." And when the crowned couple is taken around the special analogion table three times, three hymns are sung, revealing the meaning of the crowns.[115]

In Marriage, we are given the possibility of establishing a new home that can reveal the Kingdom of God. And if we choose to make it so, our dinner table can become a manifestation of the Heavenly Banquet Table and be transformed from its mere utilitarian function into an altar of grace.

## *A Word to my Children*

Your mother and I have been married now for 25 years. When we celebrate, we celebrate with wine. I have a hard time celebrating anything without your mother; my life would be

---

[112] Alexander Schmemann, Liturgy and Life (The Department of Religious Education of the Orthodox Church in America), p. 104
[113] Ephesians 5:32. Some say the whole idea of sacrament is not in the Bible, but the Greek word for "mystery," translated into Latin as "sacrament" is right here in this verse.
[114] This takes place in the Orthodox Christian Service of Holy Matrimony.
[115] ibid. p. 104. The "analogion" is a table set out in the Nave of the Church and used, instead of the Altar, as the place for conducting the Service of Marriage. The three hymns sung during this triple procession are as follows:
O Isaiah, dance thy joy, for a virgin is with child. And hath borne a son, Immanuel, both God and Man and holy is His Name, Whom magnifying, we call the Virgin blessed.
Ye holy martyrs, who fought the fight and have revealed your crowns, entreat ye the Lord that He will have mercy on our souls.
Glory to thee, O Christ our God, the Apostles boast of Thee—the joy of the martyrs, whose preaching was the consubstantial Trinity.

boring without her and this is one reason, among many, I married her. I can't really enjoy wine without her; there's something about sharing a meal together with a glass of wine that manifests and restores our love for each other, stops all quarrels and allows forgiveness to break through the walls and barriers of this fallen world. Fr. Alexander says:

> Men understand all this instinctively if not rationally. Centuries of secularism have failed to transform eating into something strictly utilitarian. Food is still treated with reverence. A meal is still a rite—the last "natural sacrament" of family and friendship, of life that is more than 'eating' and 'drinking.' To eat is still something more than to maintain bodily functions. People may not understand what that 'something more' is, but they nonetheless desire to celebrate it. They are still hungry and thirsty for sacramental life.[116]

You know that your mother and I have not always treated each other as "king" and "queen," neither have we consistently succeeded at creating such an atmosphere in our home, but you also know, that our steadfast commitment to each other through thick and thin have kept us coming back to our family table time and time again.

The crowns received in marriage are also the crowns of martyrdom, and any marriage, if it is to mature, requires an acceptance of the Cross. Jesus said:

> If anyone desires to come after Me, let him deny himself, and take up his cross daily, and follow Me. For whoever desires to save his life will lose it, but whoever loses his life for My sake will save it. Luke 9:23-24

Your mother and I have a long way to go on a journey that is not yet complete, in a marriage that does not yet perfectly manifest the Kingdom. But we're still working on it; we're still moving forward hand in hand, still looking ahead with positive anticipation. I like Fr. Alexander's description of the beauty of marriage:

> In movies and magazines the "icon" of marriage is always a youthful couple. But once, in the light and warmth of an autumn afternoon, this writer saw on the bench of a public square, in a poor Parisian suburb, an old and poor couple. They were sitting hand in hand, in silence, enjoying the pale light, the last warmth of the season. In

---

116 Alexander Schmemann, *For the Life of the World*, (Crestwood, N.Y.: St. Vladimir's Seminary Press, 1973), pp. 15-16.

*silence: all words had been said, all passion exhausted, all storms at peace. Their whole life was behind—yet all of it was now present, in this silence, in this light, in this warmth, in this silent unity of hands. Present—and ready for eternity, ripe for joy. This to me remains the vision of marriage, of its heavenly beauty.*[117]

God willing, your mother and I will have many more years of married life together. My prayer is that we may spend what time God grants us to the fullest and in the words of your dearly departed Grandpa Finley, "Greet the end of our way with faith and exit this life gracefully."[118]

*John David Finley and Janet Lynn Morrison*
*Married on July 19, 1980*
*in Santa Barbara, California*

[117]Alexander Schmemann, For the Life of the World, (Crestwood, N.Y.: St. Vladimir's Seminary Press, 1973), p. 90.

[118] My brother, Howard quoted one of my Dad's final spoken prayers on his deathbed as follows: "Dear Lord, it seems that Fanneita (my mother) and I have come to the end of our way. Help us to greet it with faith and exit this life gracefully."

# CHAPTER 11 ~ *Oil to Make His Face Shine*

Do you know what the word "Christ" means? The Anointed One. Anointed with what? Olive oil. After the Great Flood, Noah sent out the dove twice to see if the water had subsided. The second time, the dove came back to him in the evening, and there in its beak was a freshly picked olive leaf. From this we see the first instance of the olive tree, its leaves, fruit and oil as a manifestation of God's mercy and reconciliation with mankind.

We read in the book of Exodus that the Lord commanded Moses to make a sacred anointing oil from olive oil, the finest spices, liquid myrrh, cinnamon, aromatic cane and cassia. With it, He instructed Moses to anoint the tent of meeting, the Ark of the Covenant, the table and its utensils, the altar of incense, the altar of burnt offering with all its utensils and the basin with its stand. In addition, he commanded Moses to anoint Aaron and his sons, and consecrate them, in order that they might serve the Lord as priests.[119]

Samuel took the horn of oil, and anointed David in the presence of his brothers; and the Spirit of the Lord came mightily upon David from that day forward.[120]

Prophesying of Jesus Christ, the Psalmist says:

> *Your Throne, O God, is forever and ever; a scepter of righteousness is the scepter of Your kingdom. You love righteousness and hate wickedness; Therefore God, Your God, has anointed You with the oil of gladness more than Your companions.* Psalm 44(45):6-7

This passage proclaims Christ (the Messiah) as God, not simply a human deliverer. In fact these very same words are quoted in St. Paul's letter to the Hebrews as God the Father saying to

---

[119] Ex. 30:22-30. See also Leviticus 8:10-30
[120] I Sam. 16:13. See also Psalm 22(23):5 and Psalm 88(89):19-21.

His Only-Begotten Son: "Your throne, O God...."[121] These and other stories and scripture passages in both the Old and New Testaments help us to understand more deeply what it means that Jesus is the Christ, the Anointed One.

Do you know the Greek word for oil, "eleos," is the same root word for mercy? What about the Italian word "olio?" It too, is from the same root word. When we sing "Kyrie eleison" in Church, we are singing "Lord, have mercy." Oil and mercy go together.

## *The Mystery of Grace*

The Prayer of the Anointing Oil (made from olives of course) used in the Service of Baptism recalls the story of Noah and the dove and asks that through the anointing, the Lord have mercy on those who are about to be baptized:

> *O Lord and Master, the God of our fathers, Who didst send unto*
> *them that were in the ark of Noah Thy dove, bearing in its beak a*
> *twig of olive, the token of reconciliation and of salvation from the*
> *flood, the foreshadowing of the mystery of grace; and didst provide*
> *the fruit of the olive for the fulfilling of Thy Holy Mysteries; Who*
> *thereby fillest them that are under grace: Bless also this holy oil with*
> *the power, and operation and indwelling of Thy Holy Spirit, that it*
> *may be an anointing unto incorruption, an armour of righteousness,*
> *to the renewing of soul and body, to the averting of every assault of*
> *the devil, to deliverance from all evil of those who shall be anointed*
> *therewith in faith, or who are partakers thereof; unto Thy glory and*
> *the glory of Thine Only-Begotten Son, and of Thine all-holy, and*
> *good, and life-giving Spirit: now and ever, and unto ages of ages. Amen.*

This Oil of Gladness is first poured into the baptismal water before the person is anointed on the forehead, chest and back, ears, hands and feet. We do this because our reconciliation in baptism is not only with God, but also with our fellow man and the whole created cosmos of which water is the prime element.

And when we are immersed three times in the Name of the Father and of the Son and of the Holy Spirit, and raised up to newness of life from this liberating water grave, we are clothed with the Garment of Righteousness, the Robe of Light, and anointed with yet another oil from the olive, the Holy Chrism. Yes, we become the "Anointed Ones," who shine with "The seal of the gift of the Holy Spirit."

By virtue of our union with Christ, the Anointed One in Holy Baptism and having

---

[121] Heb 1:8-9

received the seal of the Holy Chrism, we are made to share in the Royal Priesthood and are granted participation in the Holy Body and Precious Blood of our Lord and God and Savior Jesus Christ. This establishes the beginning of the Christian Life.

## *Olive Oil as a Healing Remedy*

The Apostles often anointed the sick with oil: "...and they cast out many devils, and anointed with oil many that were sick, and healed them."[122]

All of us have been wounded to one degree or another by the fallen condition of this temporal life. We all know people who have at times in their lives entered into the depths of despair and sorrow and stared death in the face.

We are all familiar with the story of the Good Samaritan who came upon a man, robbed and wounded, lying helpless on the side of the road.[123] The Good Samaritan bound up his wounds and carried him to a haven of rest where he could be healed.

The man beside the road is an image of each one of us, and the wounds and the loss of this man, the image of our own sins and of those inflicted by that old robber, the Devil. The Good Samaritan is the Great Physician, our Lord Jesus Christ and the inn, the walls of the Church within which the injured receive care.

Realizing that we too have been robbed and beaten up in our lives in various ways, we acknowledge our need to be visited by the Good Samaritan, Who cleanses our wounds with oil and wine and carries us into the safe haven of the Kingdom of God in order to heal our souls and bodies. So we rejoice when the Savior finds us beside the troubled road of life and ministers to us through the priest in the Sacrament of Holy Unction.

St. James exhorts us to call for the elders of the Church when we are sick and ask for prayer and anointing with oil:

> *Is any sick among you? Let him call for the elders of the church; and let them pray over him, anointing him with oil in the name of the Lord: and the prayer of faith shall save the sick, and the Lord shall raise him up; and if he has committed sins, they shall be forgiven him.* James 5:14-15

In our service of Holy Unction (Anointing) the priest offers the following prayer over the olive oil offered for the anointing of the faithful:

> O Lord, Who through Thy mercies and bounties healest the disorders of our souls and bodies: Do Thou Thyself, O Master also sanctify this oil, that it may be effectual for those who are

---

[122] Mark 6:13
[123] Luke 10:30-37

anointed therewith, unto healing and unto relief from every passion, of defilement of flesh and spirit and every ill; and that thereby may be glorified Thine all-holy Spirit, now and ever and unto ages of ages. Amen.[124]

## Olive Oil as Light

Olive oil is also used for light. God commanded that olive oil be burned in the lamps of the Holy Place.[125] In the Parable of the Ten Virgins, five wise virgins took oil in their vessels with their lamps.[126] Even today many of the lamps used in the churches are filled with olive oil, manifesting our readiness to meet the Christ, the Bridegroom as He comes to us invisibly up borne by the angelic hosts.

## Olive Oil as Food

*For the Lord your God is bringing you into a good land, a land with flowing streams, with springs and underground waters welling up in valleys and hills, a land of wheat and barley, of vines and fig trees and pomegranates, a land of olive trees and honey, a land where you may eat bread without scarcity, where you will lack nothing, a land whose stones are iron and from whose hills you may mine copper. You shall eat your fill and bless the Lord your God for the good land that he has given you.* Deut. 8:7-10

Give me a glass of red wine, a couple of thick slices of Italian ciabatta bread with a dipping dish of olive oil sprinkled with a little balsamic vinegar and a touch of salt and pepper, and I'm happy! Seriously, this is a meal in itself.

## Olive Oil University

People living in areas around the Mediterranean Sea have very low rates of heart disease even though their diet is high in fat. Most of their dietary fat comes from olive oil. The monounsaturated fat from olives tends to lower levels of "bad" LDL-cholesterol and maintain levels of "good" HDL-cholesterol. Studies have shown that olive oil can protect arteries from building up plaque, reduce blood pressure, regulate blood sugar and help cleanse the digestive system.

It is important to note, however, that not all olive oils are created equal, so some degree of education is required. Virgin olive oils can have the following designations and classifications depending on their organoleptic[127] and analytic characteristics.

---

[124] Prayer of Oil from the Office of Holy Unction
[125] Ex. 27:20, Lev. 24:2
[126] Matt 25:4
[127] taste and aromafatty acids, not to the taste.

**Extra Virgin olive oil** has a free acidity,[128] expressed as oleic acid of not more than 1%. Extra Virgin olive oil accounts for less than 10% of oil in many producing countries. It is used on salads, added at the table to soups and stews and for dipping.

**Virgin olive oil** has a free acidity, expressed as oleic acid of not more than 2%.

**Refined (or pure) olive oil** is obtained from virgin olive oils by refining methods that do not lead to alterations in the initial glyceridic structure. It has a free acidity, expressed as oleic acid of not more than 3%.

### Obsolete or unregulated terms

"**First press**" and "**cold pressed**" are unregulated descriptions for olive oil. They refer to processes used with vertical screw or hydraulic presses. Today the vast majority of oil is made in continuous centrifugal presses. There is no first or second pressing.

The paste is almost always warmed to room temperature during the "malaxation" process before being centrifuged using horizontal decanters (olives are harvested in the winter when it is cold). This is still considered "cold pressed" according to International Olive Oil Council (IOOC) regulations, so you will often see it on labels.

"**Lite**" or "**Light.**" In the U.S., flavorless and often low quality (refined) oil is sold as "lite" or "light" oil for a premium price. The "light" designation refers to flavor, not caloric content, as all olive oil has the same amount of calories. There is no official definition of lite or light.

## Recipes using Olive Oil

Enough of the technical stuff, let's get back to the food itself and some great dishes, sauces and salads that contain this wonderful extract from the olive:

### BRUSCHETTA

2 medium French baguettes, cut into 12 slices each
1/2 large red onion, diced
4 medium garlic cloves, finely diced
1/2c extra virgin olive oil[129]
1/4c fresh basil leaves, finely chopped
1/2tsp salt
4 medium tomatoes, diced

---

[128] the degree of acidity refers to the proportion of the free fatty acid, not to the taste.
[129] I like Joelle Late Harvest Manzanillo Extra Virgin Olive Oil. www.joelleoil.com

Preheat oven to 350F. Place bread slices on an ungreased baking sheet. Bake 5 minutes, flip and bake another 5 minutes. Meanwhile, combine onion, garlic, oil, chopped basil and salt in a bowl. Mix thoroughly. Dice tomatoes, drain off excess tomato juice, add tomatoes to mixture and stir gently. Spoon mixture evenly onto bread slices and serve.

## MUFFALETTA

12oz (dr wt) jar pitted Kalamata olives (or black olive pieces)
14oz (dr wt) jar green Manzanilla olives stuffed with pimiento
1Tbl capers
4-6 anchovy fillets
juice of a lemon
2-3 garlic cloves, diced
1/2tsp black pepper
1Tbl fresh basil
1tsp oregano
1/4c extra virgin olive oil

Drain off any excess juice from the olives then mince in a food chopper or by hand. Transfer to a mixing bowl and add capers. Puree anchovy fillets with lemon juice, garlic, pepper, herbs and extra virgin olive oil in a food processor or blender. Pour over olive mixture and toss. Serve with crackers or toast points.

## POLENTA WITH MARINARA SAUCE

6c water, chicken broth or clear soup stock
1tsp salt
2c polenta (quick yellow corn grits)
1/2tsp black pepper
1tsp poultry seasoning
2tsp minced garlic
bunch green onions, chopped

Bring the water or stock to a boil in a heavy 3-quart saucepan. Add salt then slowly add the polenta, stirring constantly to avoid lumps. When mixture begins to thicken, reduce heat to a simmer and add pepper, poultry seasoning and minced garlic. Stir often for 5-10 minutes or until the polenta is thick and begins to pull away from the sides of the pot. Add chopped green onions and stir. Spread mixture into a lightly greased 9x13 baking dish and let cool until mixture has congealed.

Before serving, broil in the oven until browned on top. Cut into squares and top with marinara sauce. See recipe that follows. I like to add sliced mushrooms to the marinara before serving. Sprinkle with freshly grated Parmesan, Romano or Asiago cheese. Serves 8.

For a variation, stir in a 10oz box of frozen chopped spinach to the polenta after it is cooked. Be sure the spinach is completely thawed and drained before adding to polenta.

### MARINARA SAUCE
28oz can whole tomatoes
1/4c red wine
3 cloves, garlic crushed and finely diced
3Tbl extra virgin olive oil
1Tbl sugar
1tsp dried oregano
1/2tsp salt
1/4tsp black pepper
2Tbl fresh basil, chopped
1Tbl fresh parsley, chopped

Puree canned tomatoes in a blender. Add all remaining ingredients except fresh basil and parsley and buzz again. Pour into a 2-quart saucepan under medium heat and bring to a slow boil. Reduce heat, add fresh basil and parsley and simmer for 15 minutes. Mix into or pour over your favorite pasta.

You can add so many things to this sauce for variety: sautéed onions and green peppers, chopped mushrooms, ground hamburger—whatever you like over spaghetti.

## TOMATO MOZZARELLA SALAD (CAPRESE)
1/2lb fresh spinach and/or arugula
2 large tomatoes in 1/4" slices
6-8oz mozzarella cheese in 1/4" slices[130]
1 small red onion, sliced, separated into rings (optional)
1/4c extra virgin olive oil
2Tbl balsamic vinegar
1 garlic clove, finely minced
1-2Tbl fresh basil leaves, finely chopped
2Tbl pine nuts
 salt and black pepper to taste

---

[130] Be sure to use the softer high moisture mozzarella packed in liquid. Try to find some made from buffalo milk or a combination of cow and goat milk.

Arrange tomato and cheese slices alternately on a plate of fresh greens. Top with onion rings. Mix the oil, vinegar, garlic, and drizzle over the salad. Sprinkle with chopped basil and pine nuts. Salt and pepper to taste, then serve.

## CANNELLINI ASIAGO SALAD

1 15oz can cannellini beans, drained
1 small red onion, sliced, separated into rings
1/4c extra virgin olive oil
1Tbl fresh basil leaves
2Tbl balsamic vinegar
1 garlic clove, finely minced
 salt and black pepper to taste
1lb fresh spinach and/or arugula
4oz asiago cheese, shaved

In a large mixing bowl, combine cannellini beans, sliced red onion, olive oil, basil leaves, balsamic vinegar, minced garlic, salt and pepper. Toss thoroughly. Add greens and toss again. Arrange on salad plates and tops with shaved asiago cheese.

## COUSCOUS SALAD

1-1/2c water
1/4c extra virgin olive oil
1/2tsp salt
1-1/2c couscous
2Tbl prepared sweet mustard
1/4c lemon juice
2tsp garlic, diced
1c cucumber, chopped
1c tomatoes, chopped
1/2 onion, chopped
1/2c fresh parsley, chopped
more salt and pepper to taste

In a 2-quart saucepan, combine water, 2Tbl extra virgin olive oil and salt. Bring to boil. Remove from heat. Pour dry couscous into the saucepan. Stir well. Cover and let stand for 5 minutes. Fluff with a fork.

In a medium-sized bowl, mix the mustard, lemon juice, 2Tbl extra virgin olive oil and chopped garlic. Add cooked couscous and the chopped cucumber, tomatoes and onion to this mixture. Toss well. Add parsley and season to taste. Refrigerate before serving. Serves 6-8 as a side salad.

## MEDITERRANEAN VEGETABLE CASSEROLE

2 onions
10-12 cloves garlic
2 ribs celery
2 bell peppers (red, green, orange or yellow)
3 potatoes
2 zucchini
2 large eggplant (or 4-6 Chinese or smaller variety)
2-4 tomatoes (Roma or smaller variety)
1/2c extra virgin olive oil (or you can drown the vegetables in oil for all I care)
1/2c lemon juice
1 bunch fresh mint leaves
1/2 bunch parsley, chopped
salt to taste

Coarsely chop all vegetables and toss in oil, juice, fresh herbs and salt. Bake covered with foil in a large casserole dish at 300F for 3 hrs. Stir and recover with foil after 1-1/2 hrs.

## ZATAR PITA BREAD

Mixed Zatar is not easy to find. You're going to have to go to a Middle-Eastern or Greek market to find it. It's worth the effort. Mixed Zatar is a blend of thyme, ground sumac[131] and toasted sesame seeds.

When I was a boy growing up in Oklahoma we had to watch out for poison oak and poison sumac when we walked and played in the woods. So the first time I saw the ingredients for zatar, I thought...well you know. Anyway, it's not poison.

This blend can be mixed with olive oil until it forms into a paste. Then it is brushed onto pita bread and baked in the oven at 350-400F for about 5 minutes. You can then cut the pitas into wedges (about the size and shape of tortilla chips) if you like. Serve for dipping with hummus, baba ganouj, or simply as a side for any meal. For a change of pace, serve this for breakfast with a hot cup of coffee. Zatar is also used in marinades for chicken.

---

[131] This is commonly referred to as the "red mix." There is a "green" mix that uses wild marjoram instead of ground sumac. I like the red mix.

### HERBED FETA
1c crumbled feta cheese (about 1/4lb)
2Tbl extra virgin olive oil
1-2tsp mixed zatar
1Tbl fresh parsley, chopped

Place crumbled feta in a small mixing bowl. Add olive oil, zatar, fresh parsley, and stir gently. Serve with pita bread, scrambled eggs and a cup of coffee for breakfast. Have a little cayenne pepper sitting close by for the eggs.

### HUMMUS (CHICK PEA AND TAHINI DIP)
2-15oz cans garbanzo beans, drained
1c tahini sauce (see below)
4Tbl extra virgin olive oil
1tsp cumin
paprika, chopped fresh parsley and more olive oil

Drain garbanzo beans and add to food processor. Add tahini sauce, olive oil, cumin, and blend. Transfer to a serving bowl. Sprinkle with paprika, chopped parsley, and drizzle with a little olive oil. This is great for breakfast—a good source of protein. Serve with pita bread and Greek olives.

### TAHINI SAUCE
1/2c water
1/2c sesame tahini paste
1/2c lemon juice
1Tbl fresh parsley, chopped (optional)
1tsp garlic paste (or 3 cloves garlic minced)
salt and cumin to taste

Simply combine ingredients in a food processor and buzz! Makes approximately 2 cups.

### TABOULI (PARSLEY AND WHEAT SALAD)
1/2c fine #1 or #2 grade bulgur
1/2c lemon juice
1/2c extra virgin olive oil

2 bunches parsley, finely chopped
1/2c mint leaves (or 2-3T dried)
6 green onions, diced
1 small cucumber, diced
2 medium tomatoes, diced
salt and pepper to taste

Rinse bulgur, then mix with lemon juice and extra virgin olive oil and set aside. Wash parsley and mint. Pull leaves from stems and finely chop. Clean and wash vegetables and dice small. Combine ingredients. Add salt and pepper to taste.

## Baba ganouj (Eggplant and Tahini Dip)
2 large eggplants
3/4c tahini sauce
1/4c extra virgin olive oil
paprika, chopped fresh parsley and more olive oil
1/3c pine nuts (optional)
salt and black pepper to taste

Peel eggplant. Slice into quarters lengthwise. Lay flat in a covered baking dish in just a little water and bake at 350F for 15-20 minutes or until tender.[132] Flavor with salt and pepper. When eggplant is soft, transfer to a large mixing bowl and mash with a fork or slice eggplant into small chunks and blend in a food processor.

Add tahini sauce and extra virgin olive oil and blend into eggplant. Add 1/3c pine nuts and stir. Transfer to a serving bowl. Let is sit for a while to cool. It will congeal and develop a thicker consistency. When ready to serve, sprinkle with paprika, minced parsley and drizzle with a little more olive oil. Serve with pita bread.

## Fatayer (Spinach Pie Triangles)
1lb spinach (fresh or frozen)
1/2tsp salt
1 medium onion, finely diced

---

[132] Eggplant can also be grilled or broiled. This gives it a more smokey flavor.

2Tbl canola or extra virgin olive oil
1/4c lemon juice
1/4tsp pepper
1/2c lightly toasted pine nuts (optional)
1Tbl margarine
2 cans refrigerated biscuits (I know, I know... this is cheating)

If using fresh spinach, wash, stem, drain and chop spinach. Place it in a large mixing bowl, sprinkle with salt, and let wilt. Squeeze the spinach until all the water is removed. If using frozen spinach, thaw and then squeeze spinach until all the water is removed. Finely dice onion. Add this to spinach along with (salt) oil, lemon juice, and pepper. Mix well.[133]

Preheat oven to 375F. Take refrigerated biscuits and roll out or flatten to about a 5-inch diameter on a floured board. Put 1 heaping tablespoon of the spinach filling in the center of each biscuit.

> *Hint: shape filling into a triangle for a visual reference*
> *for the instructions which follow.*

Pull two sides together (1/3 of the circle) and pinch up to the center, making a raised seam. Do this again, leaving a raised Y on the top. Make sure to pinch the dough together tightly, so it does not open during the baking process.

Place the filled triangles on a lightly greased baking sheet and bake 15 minutes or until tops are golden brown. Refrigerator biscuits may have a temperature and baking time recommendation, so take this into consideration. Remove from oven and brush with melted margarine.

---

[133] For a variation outside of Lent, add 1/2c crumbled feta cheese to the spinach mixture.

# CHAPTER 12 ~ *Bread Which Strengthens Man's Heart*

*As a sheep He was led to the slaughter,*
*And as a spotless lamb before His shearers is silent, so He did not open His mouth.*

*In His humiliation, his justice was denied Him,*
*And who shall declare His generation.*

*For His life was taken up from the earth.*[134]

*Sacrificed is the Lamb of God, which taketh away the sins of the world, for the life and the salvation of the world."*[135]

*"And one of the soldiers pierced his side with a spear and there came out blood and water, and he who saw it bore witness and his testimony is true."*[136]

With these words, the priest prepares and removes the designated section of the Eucharistic loaf, called the Lamb, places it on the diskos[137] and pours the wine into the Chalice. The Mystical Supper is prepared and made ready to present to God in anticipation that He will give to us in return, His precious and all-holy Body and Blood for the forgiveness of sins and life everlasting. By this means, we are redeemed by the Blood of the Lamb.

---

[134] Isaiah 53:7-8
[135] John 1:29; I Cor. 5:7; I Peter 1:19
[136] John19:34-35
[137] A liturgical plate upon which the bread to be consecrated at the Altar is placed.

Since the fall of man came about through food, God has brought about the redemption of man through food. Therefore, what more appropriate theme than "food" could be found about which to write?

## *The Bread of the Presence*

In one of many accounts of the Resurrection, we find in Luke's Gospel the story of Christ's appearance to two of His followers on the road to Emmaus:

> *Now it came to pass, as He sat at the table with them, that He took bread, blessed and broke it, and gave it to them. Then their eyes were opened and they knew Him; and He vanished from their sight.*
>
> *And they said to one another, "Did not our hearts burn within us while He talked with us on the road, and while He opened the Scriptures to us?*
>
> *So they rose up that very hour and returned to Jerusalem, and found the eleven and those who were with them gathered together, saying, "The Lord is risen indeed, and has appeared to Simon!*
>
> *And they told about the things that had happened on the road, and how He was known to them in the breaking of the bread.*
>
> Luke 24:30-35

Do you believe the Lord can be known by us and reveals Himself to us in the breaking of the bread? I do. Furthermore, I believe that He nourishes and strengthens our hearts when we partake of His Body and Blood.

Even under the Old Covenant the showbread of the Tabernacle was considered holy.[138] Why was it called "showbread?" What did it "show? " What did it "reveal" if not the presence of the Lord? The word is even translated in the Revised Standard Version of the Bible as "the Bread of the Presence."[139] Whose presence if not the Presence of the Lord?

How much more, then, under the New Covenant of grace does the bread from the Holy Altar, the Bread from Heaven, the Bread of Life[140] manifest and reveal the presence of the Lord as we, with fear of God, with faith and love, draw near to receive it.

---

[138] Ex. 25:30; I Sam 21:6
[139] Matt. 12:4 - Revised Standard Version
[140] John 6:32-35

The priest pointing to the bread exclaims, "...and show this bread to be itself, the Body of our Lord and God and Savior Jesus Christ."[141] The word "show" is the same word in Greek that we often translate into English—"manifest" or "reveal." Having ascended into the heavenly Jerusalem, we cry out to Him in song as did the multitudes who took branches of palm trees and went out to meet the Lord in the Jerusalem of old, singing: "Blessed is He Who comes in the Name of the Lord. God is the Lord and has revealed Himself to us."[142]

What a privilege it is then, to be a part of this whole mystery of offering and receiving the Bread of Life from the Altar of God. This is why we should be encouraged to make it a regular practice in our lives to ask to bake the prosphora[143] loaves and offer them in the Church as our special offering and expression of love to God. At the same time we offer the bread, it is customary to submit the names of our loved ones and friends, both living and departed, asking that they especially be remembered in prayer on that day.

## PROSPHORA (EUCHARIST BREAD)
*Recipe for 2 Loaves*

1 pkg active dry yeast
2c warm water
5-6c white flour (not self-rising)
2tsp salt

1. Dissolve yeast in 1/2c warm water (105-109F) in a measuring cup or drinking glass. Allow it                to sit for a few minutes until yeast starts to foam.
2. Pour the other 1-1/2c warm water into a large mixing bowl. Add 3c flour and salt and stir. When yeast is activated (starting to foam) add to mixing bowl with one more cup of flour and stir. Form a soft ball and knead for approximately 10-15 minutes, adding more flour to the work surface as needed to prevent dough from sticking.

   *Note: Continue to knead and fold dough inside out adding a little flour each time. Dough should be very "stiff" (not at all sticky). Test by sticking your index finger into the dough and removing it without any dough sticking to your finger.*

3. Cover with a towel and set aside in a warm place to rise for one hour or until nearly doubled in bulk.

[141] from the Liturgy of St. Basil the Great, celebrated at certain times during the Church Year.
[142] Ps. 117(118):26-27; John 12:13
[143] A Greek word meaning: "that which is brought as an offering."

4. About 10 minutes before baking preheat oven to 350F.

5. Punch down the dough and knead for several minutes on a floured surface. With a rolling pin, roll out dough to about 1/2" thick. Cut out with a round object like a large Crisco or coffee can or lid top and set on a lightly floured cookie sheet. It should look like a huge biscuit! With your finger, wet the top with water and set aside. Roll out dough, cut a second time and carefully place a second layer on top of the first.[144]

6. Repeat this process to create the second loaf.

7. Lightly dust the Prosphora Bread Stamp[145] with flour before pressing. *Make sure no flour is clogged in the seal—clean out the grooves with a toothpick.* Press the bread stamp firmly into the center of the dough. Press down hard enough to impress the seal clearly then lift the stamp carefully.

   *Note: Prick around edges of seal with a toothpick to avoid creating air pockets under the seal.*

8. Bake loaves on a flat baking surface for 25-30 minutes until lightly brown on top.

9. Remove from oven and cool on racks for several hours before wrapping. Cover with a cloth in order to prevent outer crust from getting too hard. Bread should be thoroughly cooled, wrapped, and taken to the church well in advance of the beginning of the service.

## PROSPHORA (USING 5 LOAVES)

This is a custom with obvious scriptural overtones of Jesus' Miracle of the Feeding of the 5000. In larger Churches, this extra amount of bread is needed so that everyone can receive a small piece of the Blessed Bread (antidoron) from which the consecrated bread was taken.

Simply double the ingredients. Only one of the five loaves needs a second layer of dough on top. It's usually best, however, to make three double-layered loaves and two single-layered loaves. This way the pastor can choose the loaf with the best seal as the main loaf.

---

[144] This accomplishes two things: first, the chance of forming air pockets in the bread is diminished by rolling out the dough. Secondly, the double layer forms a thicker loaf, allowing the priest to cut a larger lamb for Holy Communion.
[145] This and other Christian bread stamps can be ordered online at www.prosphora.org

## *All Hallows' Eve*

Although we celebrate All Saints Day in our Church on the Sunday after Pentecost, still I have some degree of affinity and respect for the Roman observance of the same feast each year on November 1st.

I can remember a few years ago being so upset by a local newspaper article on Halloween and the controversy surrounding the contrast between the Roman Hispanic tradition of the Dia de Los Muertos and the "Happy Days" and "Harvest Festival" alternatives provided by some of our Christian brethren. So, Janni and I decided to go downtown on November 1st to see for ourselves how this Hispanic "Day of the Dead" was being celebrated.

As we walked up to the square downtown, just off La Arcada near the rear entrance to the Santa Barbara Museum of Art, we were truly amazed by what we saw: altars, candles, special breads,[146] pictures of departed friends and relatives.

"I know what this is!" I said to Janni. We knew what it meant to have a prayer altar, to light a candle, to prepare special wheat offerings in commemoration of our departed loved ones. Granted, there may have been some degree of superstition mixed in with the festivities, but the historical Christian root of the celebration was abundantly obvious to us.

Many Christians complain that the public school system has robbed us of the true meaning of Christmas, forcing us to limit our celebrations only to snow, reindeer and Jack Frost. So, we shouldn't do this to ourselves by removing all Christian content from the celebration of All Saints Day and substituting instead, cornucopia, hayrides, games and carnivals. The alternative celebrations sponsored by many churches simply remove the remembrance of the righteous saints, who have gone on before us in the faith, from the true celebration of "All Hallows Eve."

This modern approach to sanctity is just the opposite of the early Christian approach to pagan cultural festivals. For instance, the pagan feast of the Invincible Sun, which for centuries had been celebrated by the Romans around the time of the Winter Solstice (Dec. 25), was sanctified, redeemed and given its true meaning and identification with Jesus Christ, the incarnate Son of God, the Sun of Righteousness, by the 4th Century Christians. Centuries later, Christians around the world continue to celebrate the birth of Christ at Christmas on this very same day each year.

Does it seem strange then, that the early Christians would also inform and enlighten the Druid culture with the true meaning of the thin veil between the visible and invisible creation?[147] These early saints of the Church taught the Druids not only to worship the Sun of Righteousness, Christ our true God, but also how to properly acknowledge and be inspired and taught by the example of the "great cloud of witnesses"[148] and "to the general assembly

---

[146] Refer to index for Pan de Muerte recipe. This is the special bread for All Saints Day.
[147] November 1 became All Saints' Day (All Hallows' Day in England), by proclamation of Pope Boniface IV in the 7th century, a celebration of all the Christian saints. This was done to sanctify and redeem the Druid cultural festival of Samhain, also celebrated on November 1. The evening before All Saints' Day, October 31, became a holy, or hallowed, eve and thus All Hallows' Eve (later Hallow-e'en, Hallowe'en, Halloween).
[148] Hebrews 12:1

and church of the first-born who are enrolled in heaven…and to the spirits of righteous men made perfect."[149]

We lose ground in transforming our culture for good when we simply react to the sad state of affairs surrounding us and as Christians turn and run in the opposite direction. Why not charge ahead? Why not teach the true meaning of the event to our children? Why not take this opportunity to tell the stories of the courageous lives of the saints of the Church and be inspired by their memory?

In addition, let us resolve to improve the testimony of our own lives, by imitating the lives of the saints who have gone on before us to their rest. Perhaps then, the power of our quiet and consistent example of faith will become the best protection for our children from the evil spirits who would destroy us and our society.

## *Remembering our Departed Loved Ones*

The long-standing custom in our Church is to offer a mounded tray of boiled and decorated wheat berries on the fortieth day after the death of the person commemorated and on anniversaries of his or her death. After all, the day of the death of saints is called their "heavenly birthday."

You will recall in an earlier chapter I mentioned that my grandparents on the Bomar side used to take me, on occasion, to visit Uncle Clark's grave at the Ardmore Cemetery. Uncle Clark was my mother's big brother. She absolutely adored him. He was her hero.

Born in 1916, Clark Tyson Bomar was an outstanding young man in every way. One of his favorite activities was sandlot football. Unfortunately, a weak knee that he seemed to re-injure often, developed into cancer, inaugurating a very difficult journey, which would ultimately lead to his death at an early age.

After exhausting every possibility of saving his leg, doctors finally concluded that Uncle Clark would have to have it removed. He accepted the remedy of course, and not only learned to walk again with a wooden leg, but also learned to fly an airplane. Given the climate of the times, the family history of military service to our country, Uncle Clark desper-

*Clark Tyson Bomar
my uncle
b. Nov. 23, 1916 d. Aug. 20, 1944*

ately wanted to enlist as a soldier in World War II. He was turned down because of his physical disability.

---

[149] Hebrews 12:23

In the meantime, his cancer returned, this time into one of his lungs. My grandmother drove him all the way from Ardmore, Oklahoma to Memphis, Tennessee for one of the first lung removal surgeries in the United States. It didn't stop the cancer, which spread and eventually took his life in the summer of 1944. My mother, at the age of 23, was devastated along with Grandma and Grandpa Bomar and their foster daughter, Margaret Parks (Scarboro).

At the time of his death, family and friends were gathered in the home to pray, offer comfort and keep vigil. As is often the case, when death approaches for people of faith, Uncle Clark was doing most of the comforting. Many asked why God would take someone who was so greatly loved, who seemed to have such a promising future, Uncle Clark would respond, "We're not to ask why." He was also quoted asking, as death approached, "Do you hear that music?" "No, what does it sound like?" He said, "Like nothing you've ever heard!"

After his death, Grandma Bomar shared with my mother how she was comforted by a sense of Uncle Clark's presence at various times and in different ways. My mother has shared with me similar feelings of her own. The veil between the visible and invisible creation is indeed thin.

## In the Bosom of Abraham

In 1986 another untimely death struck our hearts when at the age of 3-1/2, my nephew, Thomas Harper Finley, was tragically killed in an automobile accident over Memorial Day Weekend. Without question, the saddest moment of my life came when I stepped onto the sidewalk leading to my brother's house in Nashville, Tennessee and saw the face of a man who had just lost his first-born son. I will go to my grave with that grief, that feeling of emptiness, that sense of loss I felt for my brother and my sister-in-law, Mary Harvey. To this day, I'm sure they still quietly carry that grief to a much greater degree than you or I will ever know.

During those few days I had with my brother, his wife and their newborn second son, Clark, Owen shared with me a verse from the Old Testament that he felt God had given him to deal with this tragedy in his heart: "... I shall go to him, but he will not return to me."[150]

In the weeks following, I was able to reflect on that verse and compose a letter to try and comfort him in his sorrow. Actually, the quiet demeanor and deep Christian faith that Owen and Mary have displayed over the subsequent years have brought me more comfort than I have ever given them. Nevertheless, I would like to share much of what I said to him in a letter dated June 29, 1986:

> *I believe that there are at least three ways in which we can go to Thomas. The first is built upon a scene in the life of Christ Himself. When Mary came to Jesus after her brother Lazarus had died, He was deeply moved and said, 'Where have you laid*

---

[150] II Samuel 12:23 King David uttered these words when the Lord struck David's first child born from Bathsheba with a sickness that resulted in the infant's death.

*Him'?*[151] *And they took Him to Lazarus' tomb where Jesus wept, but also where He demonstrated His power over death.*[152] *I believe that it is appropriate (in imitation of Christ) to go to Thomas by going to the place where he is laid; not simply to weep, (although that too is what Christ did) but more importantly, to express our faith and hope in the Resurrection, since on the Last Day, our mortal bodies will be raised to immortality*[153] *and we shall see God in our flesh*[154] *face to face.*[155] *I particularly love John 6:35-58. Three times in this passage Christ proclaims "...and I will raise him up on the Last Day."*[156]

*To sum up, I believe that it is a good and devout practice, and an expression of faith and hope in the Resurrection to visit the graveside on the anniversaries of a person's birth and death, on religious holidays such as Christmas and Easter, on Memorial Day and other such days.*

*Secondly, I believe that we can go to Thomas spiritually in worship and in prayer. I believe that Thomas is numbered among "...the great cloud of witnesses surrounding us" mentioned in Hebrews 12:1-2. This is not a physical place,*[157] *but a spiritual place, Mt. Zion, the city of the Living God, the heavenly Jerusalem, inhabited by God, the angels and "the spirits of righteous men made perfect."*[158]

*In Hebrews 9:11-12 we see that Christ entered through the greater and more perfect tabernacle obtaining eternal redemption for us. If we believe that this tabernacle is the same spiritual place mentioned in Heb. 12:22, then we can enter that holy place with Christ by virtue of our union with Him.*[159] *I believe that we enter into this heavenly and invisible place fundamentally in corporate worship,*[160] *by faith,*[161] *in order to show gratitude to God in worship*[162] *[This can also be experienced in a measure in our individual rule of prayer.] I also believe that the content of this worship includes remembering the righteous.*[163] *The following verses from Proverbs and Psalms also support this view, "The memory of the righteous is blessed,"*[164] *and*

---

[151] John 11:34
[152] John 11:43-44
[153] I Cor. 15: 20-58
[154] Job 19:23-26
[155] I Cor 13:12
[156] John 6:40, 44, 54
[157] Heb. 12:18
[158] Heb. 12:22-23
[159] Heb 10:19-20
[160] Heb. 12:25
[161] Heb. 11:1-3
[162] Heb 12:28-29
[163] Heb 11:4-40
[164] Prov. 10:7

*"Praise the Lord, How blessed is the man who fears the Lord...the righteous will be remembered forever.*[165]

*To sum up, I believe that Heb 9:11-12:29 is one long progression teaching us about worship, that by faith we can enter into the heavenly Holy of Holies in worship, and that Thomas is there with the angelic host and all the righteous, worshipping God together.*

*Thirdly, I believe that if we fight the good fight, finish the course, and keep the faith then we too will inherit a crown of righteousness on that day.*[166] *Certainly, the events of recent weeks have increased our love for His appearing since our hope now includes reunion with Thomas.*

*I'm sure you've heard the saying, "Some people are so heavenly minded they are of no earthly good." I have often heard Fr. Gordon Walker say, "Some people are so earthly minded they are of no heavenly good." I want to be numbered among the heavenly minded, as I'm sure you do. Perhaps the only way to be of any earthly good is to first become heavenly minded.*

*I hope this letter has been of some encouragement to you. It's been therapeutic for me just to recall the things I believe and write them down. Thomas' death has made me more heavenly minded, and I pray that I will be of some earthly good as a result. Perhaps that was a part of his 3-1/2 year ministry in this life—to make us more heavenly minded, and to teach us what true joy and innocence really are. If that be the case, then I say to Thomas, "Mission accomplished—well done thou good and faithful servant." May his memory be eternal!*

*With love from your brother,*

*John David*

---

[165] Psalms 112(113):1-6
[166] II Tim. 4:7-8

*Thomas Harper Finley*
*b. Nov. 17, 1982 d. May 23, 1986*

*When death takes children from our arms,*
*They gain release from all that harms;*
*They take no part in evil ways;*
*And parting young from life on earth,*
*Take leave of everything perverse,*
*To enter heaven's glorious rest,*
*And live with all the joyous blest;*
*There in the lap of Abraham,*
*In that bright, mystic holy land,*
*They join in happy choirs divine,*
*Composed of children pure and fine,*
*To sing the praise of God most high,*
*Who in His mercy drew them nigh,*
*And saved them pure from earthly sin,*
*To ever live and be with Him.*

Jack N. Sparks - June 1, 1986

## *A Grain of Wheat*

How can we as Christians endure such pain? How can we suffer the death of a loved one and somehow find life again? How can we keep the faith and carry such sorrow? We are taught in the scriptures that the Lord Himself was "A man of sorrows and acquainted with grief...surely He has borne our griefs."[167] He comforts us in ways beyond our understanding.

Jesus said of His own Death, Burial and Resurrection, "Unless a grain of wheat falls into the ground and dies, it remains alone; but if it dies, it produces much grain."[168] In another place, St. Paul exhorts us:

> *And what you sow, you do not sow that body that shall be, but mere grain—perhaps wheat or some other grain...The body is sown in corruption, it is raised in incorruption. It is sown in dishonor; it is raised in glory. It is sown in weakness; it is raised in power. It is sown a natural body; it is raised a spiritual body. There is a natural body, and there is a spiritual body.*
>
> I Cor. 15:37, 42-44

Therefore, when we come to the Church to offer the Wheat Tray in memory of those we love but see no longer, we stand in the long train of our Christian predecessors who, inspired by these Biblical images maintained in this manner, that inseparable communion with the saints of God who have gone on before us in the faith. And as we partake of the wheat after it is offered, our hearts are truly strengthened as we bear witness to the testimony of their lives and of their prayers that keep us in the Body of the Faithful.

## KOLIVA (WHEAT TRAY FOR MEMORIAL SERVICES)

*This recipe can be doubled for larger congregations*

1.5lb soft white wheat berries

1/2lb walnuts (or pecans), chopped

1 box Zwieback or graham cracker crumbs, ground

1/2lb golden raisins

1/2c granulated sugar

1-1/2tsp cinnamon

1/2tsp salt

1/8tsp ground cloves

2Tbl parsley, finely chopped (optional)

1/2lb powdered sugar

blanched almonds

yogurt-covered or white Jordan almonds

[167] Isaiah 53:3-4
[168] John 12:24

**First day of preparation** Place wheat in a large pot or Dutch oven and cover with water. Bring to a boil; cover, lower heat and simmer three hours or until tender, stirring often. Add more water while cooking if necessary. Drain. Place colander under running cold water to rinse wheat. Allow to drain thoroughly. To dry wheat, spread on double thickness of cloth on a large table. With wooden spoon, stir wheat occasionally to separate kernels. Cover with another cloth and leave overnight.

**Second day** Grind walnuts and 1/2 box of Zwieback or graham crackers. Combine with wheat, raisins, sugar, cinnamon, salt, ground cloves and parsley. Line a large silver tray with white paper doilies, extended beyond rim, and with a small portion of the wheat mixture, secure the position of the doilies. Carefully add the remaining mixture, shaping and pressing into a large mound.

Crush the other 1/2 box of Zwieback or graham crackers, and spread over wheat to cover completely. Sift 1/4lb powdered sugar evenly over the entire surface, then place a sheet of waxed paper over it and press gently to make firm. Sift and sprinkle the other 1/4lb powdered sugar evenly over top for a soft snowy appearance. Decorate with almonds, making a cross in the center banked by initials of the deceased. Accent the border of the tray with white Jordan or yogurt-covered almonds.

*Note: practice forming the cross and initials on a plate or cutting board before placing them on the wheat tray.*

## ARTOKLASIA (ARTOS BREAD FOR FEAST DAYS)

1 pkg active dry yeast
2c warm water
3/4c sugar
1/4c canola oil
2tsp salt
1tsp cinnamon (or pumpkin pie spice)
5-6c all-purpose flour

1. Dissolve yeast in 1/2c warm water (105-109F) in a measuring cup or drinking glass. Allow it to sit for a few minutes until yeast starts to foam.
2. Pour the other 1-1/2c warm water into a large mixing bowl. Add sugar, canola oil, salt, cinnamon, 3c flour, and stir. When yeast is activated (starting to foam) add to mixing bowl with one more cup of flour and stir. Form a soft ball and knead for approximately 10-15 minutes, adding more flour to the work surface as needed to prevent dough from sticking.

*Note: Continue to knead and fold dough inside out adding a little flour each time. Dough should be very "stiff" (not at all sticky). Test by sticking your index finger in the dough and removing it without any dough sticking to your finger.*

3. Cover with a towel and set aside in a warm place to rise for one hour or until nearly doubled in bulk.
4. About 10 minutes before baking preheat oven to 350F.
5. Punch down the dough and knead for several minutes on a floured surface. With a rolling pin, roll out dough to about 1/2" thick. Cut out with a round object like a large Crisco or coffee can or lid top and set on a lightly floured cookie sheet. It should look like a huge biscuit!
6. Repeat this process to create the other four loaves.

*Note: There is a special bread stamp[169] for the Artos Bread. To seal the Artos Bread, use the same technique as described in the Prosphora recipe.*

7. Lightly dust the stamp with flour before pressing. Make sure no flour is clogged in the seal—clean out the grooves with a toothpick. Press the bread stamp firmly into the center of the dough. Press down hard enough to impress the seal clearly then lift the stamp carefully.
8. Bake loaves on a flat baking surface for 25 minutes until brown on top.
9. Remove from oven and cool on racks for several hours before wrapping. Cover with a cloth in order to prevent outer crust from getting too hard. Bread should be thoroughly cooled, wrapped, and taken to the church before the service begins.

[169] Order from www.prosphora.org

# THE EUCHARIST IS...

*A poetic compilation of quotations from*
*the Rt. Rev. Protopresbyter Alexander Schmemann*
*By John D. Finley*

*The Rt. Rev. Alexander Schmemann*
*b. Sep. 13, 1921 d. Dec. 13, 1983*

**The Eucharist is a mystery...**

> ...the very mystery of joy, the mystery of all mysteries, the mystery of the Church.

**The Eucharist is a joyous gathering...**

> ...of those who are to meet the risen Lord and to enter with him into the bridal chamber.

**The Eucharist is an action...**

> ...by which a group of people become something corporately which they had not been as a mere collection of individuals.

> It is the essential attitude and the essential act of the Church, which is the new Humanity, restored by Christ ...one transforming act and one ascending movement.

**The Eucharist is a procession...**

> ...of the Church following the Ascension of Christ. (Hebrews 9)

**The Eucharist is a journey...**

> ...of the Church into the dimension of the Kingdom.

**The Eucharist is a real separation from the world...**

> We always want to make Christianity "understandable" and "acceptable" to this mythical "modern" man on the street. And we forget that the Christ of whom we speak

is "not of this world," and that after His resurrection He was not recognized even by His own disciples. We do not realize that we never get anywhere because we never leave any place behind us.

## The Eucharist is an entrance of the Church into the joy of its Lord...

...and to enter into that joy, so as to be a witness to it in the world, is the very calling of the Church, its essential ministry, the mystery by which it "becomes what it is."

It is an entrance into the risen life of Christ...the very movement of the Church as passage from the old into the new, from "this world" into the "world to come."

## The Eucharist is a manifestation of the Word of God...

God will speak to us, His eternal Word will be given to us again and we will receive it.

## The Eucharist is a movement...

...the movement that Adam failed to perform, and that in Christ has become the very life of man:

...a movement of adoration and praise in which all joy and suffering, all beauty and all frustration, all hunger and all satisfaction are referred to their ultimate End and become finally meaningful.

It is real life, a movement of love and adoration toward God, the movement in which alone the meaning and the value of all that exists can be revealed and fulfilled.

## The Eucharist is an offering...

It is our offering to Him of ourselves, of our life and of the whole world.
"To take in our hands the whole world as if it were an apple!" said a Russian poet.

## The Eucharist is a sacrifice...

...but it is the most natural act of man, the very essence of his life.

Man is a sacrificial being, because he finds his life in love, and love is sacrificial: it puts the value, the very meaning of life in the other and gives life to the other, and in this giving, in this sacrifice, finds the meaning and joy of life.

It is indeed a sacrifice offered on behalf of all and for all.

## The Eucharist is Christ Himself…

The Eucharist is His Eucharist and He is the Eucharist. "…it is He who offers and it is He who is offered."

Christ is the perfect man, Who stands before God.

Christ alone is the perfect Eucharistic Being.
He is the Eucharist of the world.

In and through this Eucharist the whole creation becomes what always was to be and yet failed to be.

## The Eucharist is the memorial of Christ…

It is the mystery of cosmic remembrance: it is indeed a restoration of love as the very life of the world.

Remembrance is an act of love.

God remembers us, and His remembrance; His love is the foundation of the world.

In Christ, we remember.

The Church in its separation from "this world," on its journey to heaven, remembersthe world, remembers all men, remembers the whole creation, and takes it in love to God.

We remember His life, His death, His resurrection: one movement of sacrifice, of love, of dedication to His Father and to men—this is the inexhaustible content of our Remembrance.

**The Eucharist is the "lifting up" of our offering...**

...and of ourselves.

**The Eucharist is the Ascension of the Church to heaven...**

We have entered the Eschaton[170], and are now standing beyond time and space; it is because all this has first happened to us that something will happen to bread and wine. It is our Ascension in Christ.

**The Eucharist is the state of perfect man...**

When man stands before the throne of God, when he has fulfilled all that God has given him to fulfill, when all sins are forgiven, all joy restored, then there is nothing else for him to do but to give thanks.

When a man stands before God face to face, when he has been accepted into this Presence, when his sins are forgiven and he has recovered his pristine beauty, the Eucharist—thanksgiving, adoration, worship—is truly the ultimate and the total expression of his whole being.

It is the Divine element, the Image of God in us, the life of paradise, the one essential relationship with God, the only full and real response of man to God's creation, redemption and gift of heaven.

It is a new style of life, the only real life of creation with God and in God, the only true relationship between God and the world.

In sin, man has lost that pure Eucharist. He has directed his life, his love, his care to wards other objects; he has become incapable of Eucharist, i.e. thanksgiving, which is the state of man in paradise.

**The Eucharist is the "breakthrough"...**

...that brings us to the table in the Kingdom, raises us to heaven, and makes us partakers of the divine food.

---

[170] A Greek word meaning "The Age to Come."

**The Eucharist is the end of the movement...**

We are at the paschal table of the Kingdom. The end of the journey, the end of time.

It is the arrival at a vantage point from which we can see more deeply into the reality of the world.

**The Eucharist is the mystery of unity and the moment of truth...**

The very expression and edification of the Church.

Here we see the world in Christ, as it really is, and not from our particular and therefore limited and partial points of view.

**The Eucharist is communion with the whole Church...**

It is the supreme revelation of the "Communion of the Saints" of the unity and interdependence of all the members of the body of Christ.

It is judgment and condemnation to people who do not see Christ in the Church, but see in it merely human pride and arrogance, selfishness and the spirit of "this world."

It is the breaking of the bread...the one source of life that brings all to it and redeems the unity of all men under one Head—Christ...the mystery of forgiveness...the mystery of reconciliation achieved by Christ and eternally granted to those who believe in Him.

It is the essential food of the Christian, strengthening his spiritual life, healing his diseases, affirming his faith, making him capable of leading a truly Christian life in this world...the gift of eternal life, an anticipation of the joy, peace and fullness of the Kingdom, a foretaste of its light.

It is both partaking of Christ's suffering, the expression of our readiness to accept His "way of life" and sharing in His victory and triumph...a sacrificial meal and a joyful banquet.

His Body is broken and His blood is shed, and partaking of them, we accept the Cross. Yet "by the Cross joy has entered the world," and this joy is ours when we are at the Lord's Table.

It is given to me personally in order to transform me into a "member of Christ" to unite me with all those who receive Him, to reveal the Church as a fellowship of love.

**The Eucharist is the mystery of the Kingdom...**

...the fullness and manifestation of the Church as the age to come.

**The Eucharist is our secret joy and certitude...**

...the source of inspiration and growth, the victory that overcomes evil, the Presence that makes our whole life—life in Christ.

**The Eucharist is the beginning...**

...and things that were impossible are again revealed to us as possible. The time of the world has become the time of the Church, the time of salvation and redemption.

# CHAPTER 13 ~ *And There is That Leviathan*

What would the world be without fishermen? Certainly there would be no Christianity. Of the twelve Apostles, Peter, James and John were all fishermen. My grandfather was a fisherman too. Like them, I love to fish. Even better, I love to catch fish.

My first recollection of a productive day of fishing was with my Grandpa Finley on McAlester Lake No.2. Lake McAlester was the main lake, but Lake No.2 was a smaller secondary reservoir used for the local water supply. I was only about five or six years old. We fished from the bank with a long cane pole, a red and white plastic "bobber," a lead weight and a small hook for red mealworms. I must have caught 50 perch that day, one after another. We threw the really small ones back, but kept the larger ones for dinner. That early experience of success on the lake penetrated my heart and soul. Not unlike a fish, I was "hooked!"

Popo was a bass fisherman. Since we didn't have a boat, our methods were limited to what we could accomplish from the bank. We occasionally fished the public lakes near McAlester, but mainly private ponds on ranch land. My grandfather knew most of the local ranchers from his many years in McAlester and his business dealings with them at the bank and through his insurance business. Because he had helped them all at one time or another, no one would refuse him when he asked if he could bring his grandsons to fish their private ponds.

Needless to say, these ponds were great places to fish. We never got "skunked." Our most productive method was live minnows on a cane pole. This would allow us (from the bank) to reach just outside the weed lines and lily pads.

I would find a rock or stump to sit on and just watch that big red and white plastic bobber dance on top of the water. I knew the minnow was alive and fresh. Then suddenly, wham! The bobber disappeared under the water with a big "pop" and the line went tight. We would fight the fish just enough to tire them, then with one big swoop of the cane pole, land them on the bank.

On my sixteenth birthday, I got an Eagle fly rod, figuring I could reach about as far as a cane pole could reach, but have a lot more fun with the fish in the fight. I know bass-fishing farm ponds in Oklahoma with live minnows on a fly rod sounds bizarre, but it worked and I had a lot of fun with it. These ponds were sometimes full of turtles and snakes that preyed on stringers of fish, so we had to keep an eye on them while in pursuit of the next keeper bass.

The whole fishing experience was a type of journey, from the preparations made the evening before, to setting the alarm, getting up before first light, breakfast in the dark, the drive to the country, stopping on the way for live minnows, parking the car, the walk to the pond, the fishing, the catching, packing up, the drive home, eating a Hershey bar, recalling how each bass took the bait and how it fought, the cleaning process, the cooking and eating.

Popo gutted and skinned the fish, leaving them whole. When I was in high school, though, my next-door neighbor, Bob Brumley, taught me how to fillet fish. I remember one time when he had come home from fishing with another neighbor, and had about 100 crappie taken from the slack water of Lake Eufaula. I watched him begin to clean all these fish. He didn't want them all and told me I could have everything I cleaned. He was using an electric knife to fillet the fish and I was using a fillet knife. Needless to say, with electricity and more experience he was much faster, but I did learn the knack

Mr. Brumley told me to roll the fillets in buttermilk and cornmeal and deep-fat fry them. He also suggested a touch of Louisiana hot sauce as a condiment. I fixed it just the way he described and the whole family loved it.

The next time I went fishing with Popo, I offered to clean the fish when we got home. I showed him my fillet knife and explained to him what Mr. Brumley had taught me. He was concerned that I would lose a lot of meat from the fish, but agreed to let me try it. Not only did I do a good job of cleaning the fish, but I cooked them according to Mr. Brumley's instructions. Popo's response; "Johnny, this is the best fish I ever ate! I guess you're never too old to learn something new." I felt proud that I had made a contribution to our fishing experience and tradition.

## FISH FILLETS (DEEP-FAT[171] FRIED)

*For a quick down and dirty method just dip the fillets in buttermilk and then cornmeal. It's really good. But if you're not in a big hurry, try this:*

all vegetable shortening
4-6 fish fillets

---

[171] If you like to deep-fry, you should invest in a small home unit with a fryer basket. They are much safer, have a built in thermostat and a self-contained unit to secure the hot oil. If you deep-fry in a pot on your stove-top, please follow these safety tips to avoid oil burns:
1) Keep children and pets out of the kitchen.
2) Keep the pot handle turned inward.
3) Use a candy/fryer thermometer to regulate the oil temperature.
4) Do not have any other projects working on the stovetop when deep-frying.
5) Do not move the pot until the oil has completely cooled.

**WET MIX**
1-1/2c buttermilk or cold water (or a 12oz beer)
2 eggs, beaten
2Tbl canola oil
2Tbl cornstarch

**DRY MIX**
1c all-purpose flour or Bisquick
1c cornmeal
1Tbl baking powder
1tsp sugar
1tsp paprika
1/4tsp pepper
1/2tsp salt

In a deep-fat fryer heat 2 inches of shortening to 350F. Cut fillets into strips no thicker than your index finger, because the coating tends to cook faster than the fish. A large fish fillet may look golden brown on the outside, and not be done (flaky) on the inside.

In a small mixing bowl combine buttermilk, eggs, oil and cornstarch. In a medium mixing bowl combine remaining dry ingredients. Let fish strips soak in the wet mixture for a few minutes, and then coat each strip thoroughly in the dry mixture.

*Note: for a thicker, crispier crust, go "dry, wet, dry." Begin by dipping the strips in the dry mixture first, then in the wet mixture and immediately again in the dry mixture.*

Fry a few at a time in order to keep the temperature of the oil relatively constant, turning once. Allow 4-5 minutes or until golden brown. Remove with tongs or slotted spoon and drain on paper towels. Serve with lemon wedges (or malt vinegar), tartar sauce, coleslaw (see index) and hush puppies.

## TARTAR SAUCE
3/4c mayonnaise
3Tbl dill pickle relish
2Tbl lemon juice (or pickle juice)
1Tbl onion, diced

1tsp prepared mustard
salt and pepper to taste

Combine all ingredients in mixing bowl. Cover and chill until ready to use.

## HUSH PUPPIES
1c cornmeal
1c flour
1Tbl baking powder
1tsp salt
1/2tsp black pepper
1 medium onion, finely chopped
6 green onions, finely chopped
1 egg, beaten
3/4c buttermilk

Mix the dry ingredients and the onions together. Blend the egg with the buttermilk and stir into the dry ingredients. You will have a very thick batter, almost like dough. If you substitute milk for buttermilk, add a little more cornmeal. Allow the batter to sit for 1/2 hour, then drop by the tablespoonful (I use a melon baller) into oil at 350F. Deep-fry until golden brown. Drain on paper towels and keep warm until ready to serve. Just for kicks, try one with a dab of prepared mustard. It tastes like a corn dog without the dog.

## *Thompson's Hole*

When I moved to Tennessee after college graduation in the spring of 1975, I didn't fish much. Then after moving to California,[172] I didn't fish much either, but I did bring my fishing gear, including my fly rod. Bass fishing in California is so much different than Oklahoma that I turned to golf instead. I like to play golf, but somehow I can't find relief in my heart and mind from the cares of this world on the golf course. On the lake, however, I can at least begin to let go.

Thus, I decided to return to fishing as my favorite pastime after suffering a severe blow in my career and in my finances. In the early 1990s the country went into an economic recession and Southern California was hit particularly hard. When people's budgets are hit hard, charitable contributions are sometimes the first thing to go.

Anyway, St. Athanasius Academy, where I taught courses in Liturgical Studies went into a financial tailspin. I lost my job in May 1992 and suddenly realized that at age 39, with a wife and three children, we were about 90 days from becoming street people.

[172]I arrived in Goleta, California on December 30, 1977.

We pulled together as a family: I found a job in the music industry, Janni went to work at Nordstrom and we shared an apartment with Janni's mother Phyllis. Emotionally and spiritually, though, I wasn't doing very well. Our pastor, Fr. Nicholas Speier, and my friend, Fr. Marc Dunaway, sensed this and made arrangements through their respective parish communities to treat our family to a two-week, all-expense-paid vacation to Alaska.

We were so excited! We started planning the trip well in advance and made contacts with friends at St. John Cathedral in Eagle River, Alaska to begin putting together an itinerary. We arrived at the Big House near the Cathedral on Monastery Road, then traveled to Denali National Park and camped with Fr. Marc and his family. We experienced such an incredible view of Denali (Mt. McKinley) that day in late August 1993. It was clear and we could see the whole mountain, something the locals told us was a rare treat.

After returning to Eagle River we began making preparations to travel down the Kenai Peninsula for a four-day fishing adventure with Tom and Joanne Webster. They had a cabin on the Kenai River. Actually it was on a small island on the river, which could only be accessed by boat. My oldest son O.J. and I drove down to meet Tom who was already there. Janni, Holly and John Charles were to come down in a couple of days with Joanne.

Although it was very late in August, it was miserably dark, cold and overcast with drizzle and light rain. The first two days, O.J. and I went upriver with Tom in search of salmon beginning their second run of the season. No such luck. We did however manage a few Rainbows, Arctic Char or Dolly Varden on each drift. The main thing I remember was how cold and wet I felt, and how very thankful I was for a good raincoat!

Janni, Holly, John Charles and Joanne arrived late that afternoon, and participated in the evening run. We did three runs per day: morning, afternoon and evening. The evening run was really quite nice; it didn't get dark until about 10:30pm, so we had plenty of time to fish. The third day was more of the same, cold, wet, no silvers, but we never came back empty-handed!

It was September 2, the last day of fishing, the last full day of our two-week vacation, and our last run, a morning run. To top it off, John Charles was celebrating his 6th birthday so we couldn't leave him behind. Tom, O.J., J.C. and I headed up the river once again. Things were different; it was a crisp, clear, calm morning. The sky was so beautiful, and there was an air of expectation: "This time maybe we'll find the silvers."

I was in front looking back on the waves made by the boat in the water. My eyes gravitated up to the treetops; I saw bald eagles flying overhead and perching in the branches. There was a light dust of high clouds and the sun shone down on the glacier water of the Kenai making it glisten like no water I had ever seen. It seemed that it had taken a full two weeks to really impact my heart and mind, but now I felt open to the future again, and I wanted to open my eyes again to what was ahead.

It felt as if I were suspended in a moment in time, maybe a moment outside of time, a moment in which I felt surrounded by the presence of God in a way all else was blotted out. My sins, my failures, my worries, all earthly cares were gone in that moment. I knew God loved my family, and I knew we loved Him. Finally, it didn't matter whether I caught a silver salmon or not, the adventure had already been a success.

"We're going to stop at Thompson's Hole. We haven't tried that spot and nobody is on it right now." Tom's voice brought me back to the task at hand. This time we anchored down. Tom seemed determined and the boys were ready to go. We baited our lines with gobs of salmon eggs, tossed them downstream and waited

It wasn't long before John Charles had a bite. He began reeling and I said to him, "You can do it, it's probably another Rainbow!" In less than a minute, John cried out, "Dad, this is really hard!" I heard the drag on his reel letting out line. My heart started to pound and I took the rod. "John, you've got a silver!" We were in business! Everyone lent a hand to land John's 10 lb. silver. What a birthday present—for all of us. We were in the hunt and the second run had begun. Tom, O.J. and I got one silver each. They were all in the 9-10 lb. range.

To this day, I can't see a salmon or eat salmon in any way, shape or form that I don't think of Thompson's Hole. God sent Noah a rainbow; He sent me a salmon. And when I eat salmon, I am always reminded of God's unfailing love, care and provision for my family, friends and every human being whom He has created. "Great is Thy faithfulness, Lord unto me."[173]

## SMOKED SALMON
2 whole salmon filets (skins on)
Brine solution
7c water
1/2c soy sauce
1/2c teriyaki sauce
1c brown sugar
1/2c salt
1tsp dill weed (optional)

[173] Great is Thy faithfulness, O God our Father,
  There is no shadow of turning with Thee;
  Thou changest not, Thy compassions, they fail not,
  As Thou hast been Thou forever wilt be.
  Great is Thy Faithfulness! Great is Thy faithfulness!
  Morning by morning new mercies I see;
  All I have needed Thy hand hath provided;
  Great is Thy faithfulness, Lord, unto me! - Thomas O. Chisholm

Combine brine ingredients in a large mixing bowl using a whisk. Add salmon fillets. Brine 8-10 hours in the refrigerator. Fish should float when sufficiently brined. Remove from brine and rinse thoroughly under running water. Pat dry.

Divide each fillet and place on smoker racks skin side down, thick pieces on the bottom rack and tailpieces on the upper rack of a Little Chief Electric Smoker. [174] Let them continue to dry for about an hour before firing up the smoker. Use alder or hickory wood chips according to smoker directions. Every two hours replenish wood chips for a total of three times. (It's possible to over do it on the wood chips.) Smoke for 8-12 hours depending on outside temperature and thickness of fillets.

Remove from smoker when fillets are completely dry and feel solid when pressed. Remove from racks. Peel off skin. Enjoy with cream cheese and bagels.

## GRILLED SALMON
2 lemons, juiced
1/2c butter or margarine, melted
1Tbl minced garlic
tarragon to taste
2 whole salmon fillets (skins on)
salt and lemon pepper to taste

Prepare Weber Grill in the usual manner using the direct method. Wash fillets and pat dry. Combine lemon juice, butter, garlic and tarragon in a small mixing bowl. When the grill is ready, lay fillets skin side down on aluminum foil.

*Hint: If you can turn up the edges on the aluminum foil to create a "pan-like" reservoir for the liquid, the coals will remain hot and the fish will simmer in the sauce and its own juices.*

Baste fillets with lemon and butter sauce, and then sprinkle with salt and lemon pepper (Lowry's seasoned salt, and/or Santa Maria Style Seasoning also work well). Place lid on grill and bake for 20 minutes or until thick end of fillets begins to flake with a fork. I usually baste them about 10 minutes into the cooking process. When they're done, just take a spatula and run it between the skin and the meat. The skin should remain stuck to the aluminum foil, leaving a skinless portion of the fillet on the spatula. Wow, this is good! Serve with rice.

[174] Visit www.luhrjensen.com for more information on the Little Chief Electric Smoker.

## SALMON CROQUETTES

15oz can salmon
1/2 lemon
2 eggs, beaten
2Tbl mayonnaise
1Tbl Worcestershire Sauce
1tsp dry mustard
2Tbl fresh parsley, chopped
2tsp Old Bay Seasoning (or celery salt)
1/2c bread crumbs (or up to 1c if using fresh bread crumbs)
1/4c canola oil (for frying)

Place salmon in a mixing bowl, adding the juice of 1/2 lemon. Combine egg, mayonnaise, Worcestershire and mustard in a one-cup measuring cup and blend thoroughly. Pour over salmon, add parsley, seasoning, bread crumbs, and stir. Shape into 6-8 patties. In a skillet, sauté patties in 2Tbl oil for several minutes until evenly browned. Add remaining 2Tbl oil a few minutes into the browning process. Remove patties and drain on paper towels.

*Note: If you're looking to cut back on oil, these croquettes can be oven broiled for 5 minutes on each side. Lightly spray the baking sheet with oil, place the croquettes on the sheet and lightly spray tops with oil.*

Garnish with lemon wedges and cocktail sauce or tartar sauce.

## *At Lake Cachuma*

My favorite time of year to fish Lake Cachuma[175] is the springtime. This is when the bass move up into the shallow flats and inlets to spawn. Their journey from the cold winter water in the depths of the lake into the warmth and light of the spring sun is not unlike our spiritual Lenten Journey, our annual pilgrimage from the depths of darkness and sin into the eternal light and warmth of the Resurrected Son.

Warmth is a manifestation of life and of the Holy Spirit, the Giver of Life. Bearing witness to this truth, the deacon (or the priest) pours the warm water into the Chalice just before Holy Communion is served, saying: "The warmth of faith, full of the Holy Spirit."

In the springtime, the bass seem vulnerable and helpless in a way. They move up into these unprotected waters according to the force of nature, clearing and guarding their shallow-water

---

[175] Lake Cachuma is located on the Santa Ynez River about 25 miles north of Santa Barbara, California on State Highway 154.

nests filled with eggs, making them easier to catch.

I am reminded of a story, though, once told by a an Orthodox Christian priest from Alaska about the attitude and approach to hunting, gathering and fishing for game among the Native American Eskimos, which may lend a different perspective on this annual cycle of life:

> *The traditional view across all of North America and Asia is that the animals are smart. They see things people can't see. They hear things people can't hear. They smell things human beings can't smell. They know things we don't know...*
>
> *This is the kind of universe you live in... so that when a hunter goes out to hunt, it's not assumed on his part (or any human being) that he's going to out-smart the animals; that's not in the picture. He can't overpower them. They are stronger and faster than he is.*
>
> *So then, philosophically, if the animals are so smart and they know so much, how come you catch them? And the traditional answer is: 'The animals allow themselves to be caught. The animal sacrifices himself to feed you. The animal dies so that you might live.*[176] *"The animals," he said, "are Christ-like creatures."*[177]

He went on to describe in the Eskimo legends a kind of contract or covenant made between the animals and the human beings:

> *If the animals agree to give themselves to the human beings in order to provide them with food or clothing, without which, of course, they would starve or die of exposure in the Arctic, in return, the human beings must be respectful and grateful and humble before the animals.*
>
> *They don't worship the animals, but they have to go about the business of hunting or gathering, even cooking in a respectful way.*[178]

As a missionary priest, I have often compared in my heart and mind the way fishermen catch fish with the way apostles or missionaries catch men. There's something to be said for desire, mentorship, the acquisition of knowledge through experience and, of course, dedication.

[176] Excerpts from a lecture delivered at the 2003 Western Region Clergy Seminar by the V. Rev. Michael Oleksa, Dean of Saint Innocent Cathedral in Anchorage, Alaska. Fr. Michael also teaches cross-cultural communication at the University of Alaska.
[177] ibid.
[178] Ibid.

Rarely does a fisherman catch the fish he sees. More often than not, fish that are caught come from the hidden depths, beyond our range of sight. It requires a degree of faith, believing the fish are there and that by properly and consistently presenting the lure or bait, in time the reward will come.

The Lord first called Andrew, but Andrew went and got his brother, Simon Peter, who later became the leader of the Apostles. In His foreknowledge, the Lord knew that Andrew would do this, but I have sometimes observed that in all my striving to raise up Christian leadership in new areas of ministry, it was actually someone else who brought the best leaders into the fold.

## *Horse Canyon*

After our most excellent Alaskan adventure in 1993, I came home with a determination to study and become intimately acquainted with the topography of Lake Cachuma and its fish habitats. It didn't take me long to realize I couldn't learn to fish this lake successfully by reading a book or watching a bass fishing video. So in the early spring of 1994 I joined the local Santa Barbara Bass Club, attended the meetings, fished a few club tournaments and learned quite a lot about the peculiarities of fishing western deep-water canyon reservoirs.

Nothing helped me more, however, than calling on a local fishing guide named Howard Bernth, to take me out and teach me how to catch a fish at Cachuma. "Howdy," as he was called by the locals, had been a lake patrolman at Cachuma for 25 years before retiring to his home at the Cachuma Village Housing Project near Bradbury Dam. More than anything else, he gave me the confidence to catch a fish, and helped me to relax and take my time on the water.

I remember once seeing Howdy at the Marina after I had purchased my own 14-foot Gregor aluminum boat from Cachuma Boat Rentals. When he asked me how I liked my new boat, I said, "Well it gets me out there where I need to be, but this Mercury 9.9 horsepower motor is really slow." "Well, who's in a hurry?" he said. Howdy's words stopped me dead in my tracks. I had forgotten why I was coming out to the lake in the first place.

I've had some awesome fish-catchin' days on the lake that truly bring back precious memories. One day, in particular, however, will live with me forever.

I was out by myself that day. It was mid-spring and the lake was full. The lake patrol had moved the log-boom way back into the upper reaches of the lake called the Narrows, allowing boaters access to a small inlet called Horse Canyon. I already had two good-sized bass in the boat when I quietly entered the canyon and worked my way back into some shallow water surrounding a large growth of tall reeds.

On two consecutive casts, one to the left of the reeds and one to the right, I caught a 4-pounder and a 3-pounder. Needless to say, I was feeling kind of "cocky" and sorry for myself at the same time. "Cocky" over what had just happened and "sorry" that there was no one but God who witnessed it.

I had to get a fifth bass into the boat so I could return to the marina with a legal limit and make my triumphant entry up to the scales at the boat dock. Suddenly the late-morning wind kicked up in typical fashion and began pushing my boat into the reeds. Because I was in very shallow water, my main motor got stuck on a log. I got out my paddle and after a considerable struggle was finally able to free myself and "rev" back from the reeds and shallow water with my trolling motor. Exhausted and unable to position the boat for fishing the reeds anymore, I decided that my limit would have to wait for another day. Perhaps I could have found another hole that day and capped off the creel with number five, but I purposefully didn't.

Looking back on it now, I'm really glad things happened the way they did that day. Sometimes the greatest spiritual lessons are learned when we fall short and have to acknowledge God's sovereignty once again. I felt the Lord telling me to relax, that I had enough fish for one day. You know, you don't always have to go for a limit of fish. After all, conservation in the watershed is a good thing.

*All we need now is five loaves*

## STUFFED FISH FILLETS — *now that's good bass!*
Carefully slice a large pocket in each of 4 large fish fillets.[179]

### SPINACH-CORNBREAD STUFFING
1/2 normal recipe of cornbread, cooled
10oz package frozen chopped spinach, thawed
1/2c diced onion
8oz can water chestnuts, drained and finely diced
1/2tsp dried tarragon
14.5oz can chicken broth

Slice cornbread (about 3c) into 1/2 inch "crouton-size" cubes. Add the spinach, onion, water chestnuts, tarragon, and mix thoroughly. Finally add enough chicken broth to make the mixture "flake" when you stir it, but "gum" when you press it.

Stuff pockets with mixture and bake in a lightly sprayed 9x13 pan (covered with foil) at 350F for 20 minutes. Remove foil and broil for 5 more minutes. Top with hollandaise sauce and garnish with a little dill weed and paprika. Serve with fresh steamed vegetables.

### HOLLANDAISE SAUCE
3 egg yolks
1/2c butter
1/2tsp lemon peel, finely shredded
4tsp lemon juice
1/8tsp salt
dash white pepper

Place the egg yolks in a blender, cover and blend for a few seconds. In a small saucepan (or microwave) heat butter together with lemon peel, lemon juice, salt and white pepper until butter is melted and almost boiling.

With blender running at high speed, and the measuring cup removed from the lid, slowly pour in the butter mixture. Blend until mixture is thick and fluffy. Serve immediately. Makes 2/3 cup.

---

[179] If it seems easier to slice all the way through the fillets and create a "sandwich" instead of a "pocket," that's acceptable.

## CHAPTER 14 ~ *The Sign of the Fish*

*Blessed art Thou, O Christ our God, who hast revealed the fishermen as most wise, having sent upon them the Holy Spirit, and through them thou hast fished the universe, O Lover of mankind, glory to Thee.*[180]

This hymn from the Feast of Pentecost shows us how life lessons can be drawn from images of fish, fishing and fishermen. The following Hymn from the Akathist Service of Great Lent echoes yet another image of the fish; this time as a silent creature:

*Ready-voiced orators we see become voiceless as fish before thee, O Theotokos, and unable to say how thou couldst give birth and yet remain virgin: but we, marveling at this Mystery, cry out in faith: Hail...*[181]

The Prophet Isaiah, foretelling the condemnation of Christ before Pilate, tells us "as a spotless lamb before His shearers is silent, so He did not open His mouth."[182] Jesus was silent like a lamb, but also like a fish.

We are told that the early Christians living under the persecution of the wicked Roman Emperors would silently draw an arch in the sand with a stick, and then hand the stick to the person opposite them to complete the sign of the fish by forming an arch in the opposite direction. Jesus is the fish— ΙΧΘΥΣ Jesus Christ, God's Son, Savior.

Several stories in the Gospels illustrate this point. I particularly love the eleven Gospel accounts of the Resurrection taken from our Sunday Matins[183] Service. Two of them speak of fish.

We read in the Gospel of Luke[184] that Jesus appeared to the disciples and said to them,

---

[180] Troparion of Pentecost
[181] Oikos 17 from the Akathist Hymn
[182] Isaiah 53:7
[183] The word "Matins" is derived from Latin word for "morning."
[184] Luke 24:36-53

"Peace be unto you." But they thought He was a ghost. Even after He let them feel His hands and feet they still did not believe. But when He asked for something to eat, they gave Him a piece of broiled fish, and in so eating and sharing it with them, He revealed His true identity as the risen Lord and illuminated their minds to understand the Scriptures and all that He had taught them.[185]

In the Gospel of John we hear that the disciples were so sad after the crucifixion of Christ and they were not yet convinced that He had risen from the dead. Peter said, "I'm going fishing" and the other disciples went with him. So they returned to their previous occupation, confused and hopeless. They didn't catch any fish all night. But when morning came, they saw a man standing on the shore telling them to cast on the other side of the boat. They didn't know it was Jesus, but when they did cast on the other side they caught 153 fish.[186]

Peter, as well as James and John, must have flashed back to a previous encounter with this Man, Christ Jesus recorded in the 5th Chapter of Luke, when three years before, Jesus had called to them after they had fished all night without success and told them to let down the nets one more time. They caught so many fish their nets were breaking.

John exploded with excitement to Peter, "It is the Lord!" Peter put on his outer garment and plunged into the sea to meet the Risen Lord. But, before they even reached the shore, Jesus had already prepared a miraculous meal for them: fish and bread. Where did this fish come from? Who caught it? Perhaps it wasn't caught, but called. We know Jesus prepared it, and when He gave it to them to eat, they knew He was the Lord.[187]

Even the fact that this "strange meal" was served on "hot coals" manifests the prophetic Eucharistic vision of Isaiah receiving the live coal in his mouth. The priest recites this verse after receiving the Body and Blood of the Lord at the Holy Altar: "Lo, this hath touched my lips, and shall take away mine iniquities and purge away my sins."[188]

Here again, Jesus used a fish to reveal His identity to the disciples. None of them dared to ask, knowing He was the Lord. After this mystical breakfast He restored Peter's leadership and called His disciples once again to continue their ministry to shepherd His flock.

With this perspective and revelation of Jesus as the Risen Lord in mind, we can now go back into a few familiar lessons from the Gospels and perhaps see them in a new light.

In Christ's Sermon on the Mount, Jesus gives His famous three-fold exhortation:

---

[185] Since thou art the true peace of God to man, O Christ, thou didst give thy peace to thy Disciples after thy Resurrection. Thou didst show them frightened when they thought that they were beholding a spirit. But thou didst remove the anxiety of their souls when thou didst show them thy hands and feet; and yet they were in doubt. But when thou didst take food with them, reminding them of thy preaching, thou didst open their minds to understand the books. And thou didst make with them the eternal covenant, blessed them, and rose, ascending into heaven. Wherefore, with them, do we worship thee, O Lord, glory be to thee (Sixth Matins Eothinon)

[186] John 21:1-14

[187] After thy descent to Hades, O Christ, and thy Resurrection from the dead, the Disciples sorrowed, as was fitting, grieving over thy removal. They returned to their occupations and attended to their nets and their ships: but there was no fishing whatsoever. But thou didst appear to them, and, since thou art Lord of all, thou didst command them to cast the nets on the right side. And at once the word became deed and they caught much fish and found a strange meal prepared for them on the ground. And thy Disciples at once partook thereof. And now, make us worthy with them to enjoy it mentally, O Lord, Lover of mankind (Tenth Matins Eothinon)

[188] Isaiah 6:7

"Ask, and it will be given you; seek and ye shall find; knock, and it shall be opened unto you; for every one that asketh receiveth; and he that seeketh findeth; and to him that knocketh it shall be opened."[189]

Then Jesus goes on to say: "Or what man is there among you who, if his son asks for bread, will he give him a stone? Or if he asks for a fish, will he give him a serpent?"[190]

Bread and fish are instruments of life while stones and serpents are, at least potentially, instruments of death. Whenever we hear the word "serpent" in the Bible, we think of the Devil. But whenever we hear the word "fish" do we think of Jesus? Or what man is there of you who, if his son asks for "Jesus" would give him the "Devil"? This is how I hear these words.

Again in the Gospel of Matthew, we read about the temple tax and the dispute over whether or not Jesus and Peter should pay this annual head tax on all male Jews twelve years old and up, except for priests and rabbis. Jesus proclaimed them to be free from this tax, but paid it anyway, not as a debt, but in consideration of their weakness and to avoid unnecessary offense. How did He do this? He instructed Peter to "go to the sea, cast in a hook and take the fish that comes up first. And when you have opened its mouth, you will find a 'piece of money;' take that and give it to them for Me and you."[191]

This coin, called a "stater" in Greek, was the exact temple tax for two. So, who paid the tax? ΙΧΘΥΣ Jesus Christ, God's Son, Savior. This same Jesus, when He hung upon the Life-giving Tree, gave His life as a ransom for many, not as a debt, but voluntarily in consideration of our weakness and because of His love for mankind.

We are all familiar with the story of the Feeding of the Five Thousand recorded in all four Gospels. We read in John 6 that Jesus multiplied the five loaves and two fish. It seems obvious to most that this miraculous meal is a remarkable preview of the Lord's Supper, the Holy Communion, the Eucharist. But what about the fish? Why the fish? What do the fish mean?

The answer, I believe, is simple. It is as we have seen before, an identification of Christ Himself. We know "what" is multiplied: bread and fish. But is this "mere" food? Do we know "Who" is multiplied, or rather Whose Body is multiplied as the "life-giving" food for the whole world? And do we know Who is the Multiplier? Jesus of course. This is the meaning of the fish.

It seems curious to me that we see in the icon of the Mystical Supper a platter or bowl in the center of the Passover table, containing sometimes a lamb, but other times, a fish. What is this fish, if not yet another identification of Christ Himself as the One of whom we partake in this heavenly banquet?

189 Matt 7:7-8
190 Matt 7: 9-10
191 Matt 17:27

## *Jonah in the Belly of the Whale*

Finally, we read in the story of Jonah that because of his disobedience to God a great tempest was sent into the sea and the sailors thought the ship might break in two. When Jonah admitted he was the cause of the storm, he asked to be thrown into the sea as a sacrifice, so that the sea might become calm again. It is noteworthy that the sailors proclaimed Jonah's innocence before casting him into the sea, and what Jonah had predicted came true; the sea ceased its raging.

Anyone who has ever been in a sea-going vessel under high winds can certainly relate to the fear that engulfed all who were on board as well as the relief provided from the calm waters through this sacrifice of "innocent blood."

We are certainly familiar with the passage in St. Matthew's Gospel where Christ identified Himself with Jonah, saying, "For as Jonah was three days and three nights in the belly of the great fish, so will the Son of Man be three days and three nights in the heart of the earth."[192]

We hear in the Prayer of Jonah from the belly of the whale, read at the Great and Holy Saturday Baptismal Service of Pascha, the same type of prophetic prayer of Jesus found in Psalm 21 (22) and Psalm 118 (119). We even hear His very words from the Cross, expressing His sense of being forsaken by God the Father, yet His complete and perfect faithfulness to God from the depths of hell:

> *I cried by reason of mine affliction unto the Lord, and he heard me; out of the belly of hell cried I, and thou hearest my voice. For thou hadst cast me into the deep, in the midst of the seas; and the floods compassed me about; all thy billows and thy waves passed over me. Then I said, I am cast out of thy sight; yet will look again toward thy holy temple. The waters compassed me about, even to the soul; the depth closed me round about, the weeds were wrapped about my head. I went down to the bottoms of the mountains; the earth with her bars was about me forever; yet hast thou brought up my life from corruption, O Lord my God. When my soul fainted within me I remembered the Lord: and my prayer came in unto thee, into thine holy temple. They that observe lying vanities forsake their own mercy. But I will sacrifice unto thee with the voice of thanksgiving; I will pay that which I have vowed. Salvation is of the Lord.*
>
> Jonah 2:2-9

---

[192] Matt. 12:40

And the word of the Lord came unto Jonah the second time, saying, "Arise..." [193]

Indeed the Lord did arise on the third day, proclaiming the Good News of the Resurrection to the world. Yet there is one other perspective that could be seen in this scene: that of Christ as the great fish. The verse introducing Jonah's prayer says, "Now the Lord had prepared a great fish to swallow up Jonah. And Jonah was in the belly of the fish three days and three nights. [194]

The question might be asked, "Who saved Jonah?" Could the answer be anything other than Christ Himself? Not only is Jonah a type of Christ, but "the Word of the Lord" also speaks to Jonah a second time, saying, "Arise."[195] Jesus is "the Word of the Lord."

The intensely humbling prayer of the priest just before the Great Entrance of the Divine Liturgy, says, "...for Thou Thyself art He that offereth and is offered, that accepteth and is distributed, O Christ our God, and unto Thee we ascribe glory." Jesus is not only our perfect savior, but also our perfect sacrifice, our accepted offering and our distributed salvation.

At the same time Jesus is like the sacrificed Jonah who remains true to His calling, so He is also like the great fish, Who rescues each of us from the depths of hell, and says to each of us, "Arise... and preach the preaching that I bid thee."

## *A New Beginning*

Fishermen, it seems, are noted storytellers, and perhaps I am no exception. But in these stories, unlike the ones told of the fish that got away, I have tried to share with you this unique story of the One Who came to save us when we had gone astray.

Someone once said there are four stages in a fisherman's life: The first stage is to catch a fish; the second stage to catch a limit of fish. The third stage is to catch a trophy fish; and the last, to simply enjoy the experience.

I haven't caught my trophy yet, but one day I know the big one, Leviathan, will rise up from the deep and break the surface of the waters. When it turns and I set the hook and feel the line spooling from the reel, I will know from the depths of my heart that I have entered into the presence of the Lord once again, and penetrated the veil of the Eschaton.[196]

193 Jonah 3:1-2
194 Jonah 1:17
195 Jonah 3:2
196 A Greek word meaning "The Age to Come."

# Appendix A — Pronunciation Guide for Wines

Barbera (Red) [bar-BEHR-uh]
Brunello (Red) [broo-NEHL-oh]
Cabernet Franc (Red) [cab-er-NAY FRAHNK]
Cabernet Sauvignon (Red) [cab-er-NAY SO-vin-yon]
Carmenere (Red) [car-men-YEHR]
Chardonnay (White) [shar-dun-NAY]
Chenin Blanc (White) [SHEN'N BLAHNK]
Dolcetto (Red) [dole-CHET-to]
Fume Blanc (White) [FOO-may BLAHNK]
Gamay (Red) [ga-MAY]
Gewurztraminer (White) [geh-VERTS-trah-mee-ner]
Grenache (Red) [greh-NAHSH]
Malbec (Red) [MAHL-beck]
Marsanne (White) [mahr-SANN]
Merlot (Red) [mur-LO]
Meritage (Red) [MER-i-tij][197]
Mourvedre (Red) [more-VAY-druh]
Muscat (White) [MUSS-kat]
Nebbiolo (Red) [NEH-bee-oh-low]
Petite Sirah (Red) [peh-TEET sih-RAH]
Pinot Blanc (White) [PEE-no BLAHNK]
Pinot Gris (Grigio) (White) [PEE-no GREE or GREE-zho]
Pinot Noir (Red) [PEE-no NWA]
Riesling (White) [REES-ling]
Sangiovese (Red) [san-geeo-VEHS-eh]
Sauvignon Blanc (White) [SO-vin-yon BLAHNK]
Semillon (White) [SEM-ih-yon]
Syrah or Shiraz (Red) [sih-RAH or shih-RAHZ]
Tempranillo (Red) [temp-rah-NEE-yo]
Viognier (White) [vee-oh-NYAY]
Zinfandel (Red) [ZIHN-fan-dell]

---

[197] A contraction of two words: merit and heritage, Meritage is a proprietary blend specific to the Americas.

Janni and I love to go wine tasting in the beautiful Santa Ynez Valley. We don't go as often as we would like, but when we can grab some time to go, we do.

The 50 miles from Point Conception to the Rincon just east of Carpinteria constitute the only east-west traverse of shoreline from Alaska to Cape Horn and the Santa Ynez and San Rafael Mountains form a unique coastal range. The east-west running valleys open up to the Pacific Ocean, which allow the inland flow of fog and ocean breezes to make this region one of the coolest viticultural areas in California. All of the classic grape varietals can be grown in Santa Barbara County due to the many microclimates.

Within Santa Barbara County there are three distinct appellations:[198] the Santa Maria Valley, Santa Ynez Valley and Santa Rita Hills, comprising more than 20,000 acres of vineyards. Wine grapes are among the most valuable crops in the county. Most of the wineries are small businesses, run by individuals or families, who make many contributions to the local community. In addition, the Santa Barbara County Vintners' Association[199] hosts special events, the proceeds of which go in part to local nonprofit organizations.

## Labels

American wine labels tell us several things. First, the growing region or viticultural area: California, Central Coast, Santa Barbara County, Santa Maria Valley, Santa Ynez Valley, Santa Rita Hills. For some, a viticultural area is a major quality tag for a wine product. This designation means very little, however, unless we know which varietal grapes a particular growing region's reputation is built upon.

There are a number of vineyards within each growing region that are well known, sometimes for a particular varietal, other times, for the overall quality of all varietals coming from that particular vineyard. If you see a vineyard designation on a label like Bien Nacido, Thompson, Valley View, or Sanford and Benedict, chances are it's a great vineyard, especially known for the varietal used in that wine.

Usually we see the varietal name of the grape used to produce a particular wine. Sometimes instead of seeing designations such as Merlot or Cabernet Sauvignon, we see something like "Cuvee" or "Meritage." These and other words are used to designate "blends" of two or more varietals when no one varietal comprises at least 75% of the content.

Some labels say "Estate" or "Estate Bottled." This means a winery is located in, and gets all of its grapes to produce a particular wine from, a common viticultural area from vineyards that it owns or controls.

---

[198] An appellation is the geographical name of a region under which a winegrower is authorized to identify and market wine. These regions are called American Viticultural Areas (AVAs) and must be "recognized" and "defined" by the Bureau of Alcohol, Tobacco and Firearms.
[199] www.sbcountywines.com

Finally, you may see "Reserve" or "Proprietor's Reserve." Legally, this doesn't mean or designate anything. Basically, it means whatever a particular winery wants it to mean. So you'll have to ask.

What follows is by no means an exhaustive list of wineries in Santa Barbara County. The groupings by area, however, will give you an idea of the varietals that grow in each area and how the various microclimates contribute to their success.[200]

## LOS ALAMOS VALLEY

*Los Alamos, which means "The Cottonwoods" in Spanish, remains a strong and successful growing region situated between the Santa Maria and Santa Ynez valleys. The Los Alamos Valley is bounded by the northern Solomon Hills and the southern Purisima Hills. Los Alamos has a temperate climate all its own, a little cooler than the Santa Ynez Valley and a little warmer than Santa Maria Valley.*

Bedford Thompson Winery & Vineyard / www.bedfordthompsonwinery.com
  Thompson Vineyard – Pinot Gris, Chardonnay, Cabernet Franc, Grenache,
    Mourvedre, Syrah, Petite Sirah
Chimere / www.chimerewinery.com
Lucas & Lewellen Vineyards (tasting room in Solvang) / www.llwine.com
  Los Alamos Valley Vineyards – 20 varietals
  Goodchild Vineyard and Old Adobe Vineyard (Santa Maria Valley) – Pinot Noir,
  Chardonnay
  Lewellen & Lucas Vineyard, (Santa Maria Valley) – Chardonnay, Pinot Noir
  and Pinot Blanc
  Valley View Vineyard (Santa Ynez Valley) Cabernet Sauvignon, Sauvignon Blanc,
  Cabernet Franc, Syrah, Petit Verdot and Malbec.
Meridian Vineyards (tasting room in Paso Robles) / www.meridianvineyards.com
  White Hills – Chardonnay, Pinot Noir
  Cat Canyon Vineyard – Chardonnay, Pinot Noir

## SANTA MARIA VALLEY

*The fog and wind-swept Santa Maria Valley boasts the longest grape growing season in California. With cool ocean breezes pouring into this area, Chardonnays and Pinot Noirs, two varietals especially amenable to this coastal influence, are the flagship wines of this region.*

---

[200] One unique exception is the Barnwood Vineyards www.barnwoodwine.com located in the Cuyama Valley of Santa Barbara County. The vineyards located at an elevation of 3200 feet have less fog and sunnier days than Santa Maria just due west. This weather is particularly well suited to Bordeaux and Rhone varietals.
  Barnwood Vineyards - Sauvignon Blanc, Chardonnay, Merlot, Cabernet Sauvignon, Zinfandel and Syrah, Cabernet Franc, Petite Syrah, Tempranillo, Viognier, Mourvedre, Grenache, and Cinsault

Brucher Winery / www.brucherwineandart.com
Cambria Winery & Vineyard / www.cambriawines.com
    Julia's Vineyard – Pinot Noir
    Katherine's Vineyard – Chardonnay
    Tepusquet Vineyard – Sangiovese, Syrah and Viognier, Pinot Blanc, Pinot Gris
    and Chenin Blanc
    Bench Break Vineyard – Chardonnay and Pinot Noir
Cottonwood Canyon Vineyard & Winery / www.cottonwoodcanyon.com
    Cottonwood Canyon Vineyard – Chardonnay, Pinot Noir, Syrah
Foxen Vineyard / www.santabarbara.com/winecountry/foxen/default.asp
    Tinaquaic Vineyard – Chardonnay, Syrah, Cabernet Franc
Presidio Winery (tasting room in Solvang) / www.presidiowinery.com
    Mission Vineyard – Chardonnay, Pinot Noir
McKeon-Phillips Winery / www.mckeonphillipswinery.com
Rancho Sisquoc Winery / www.ranchosisquoc.com
    Rancho Sisquoc Vineyards – Cabernet Sauvignon, Merlot, Chardonnay, Sauvignon Blanc,
    Riesling and Sylvaner

## SANTA RITA HILLS

*Wines from the Santa Rita Hills have also received national acclaim for Pinot Noir and Chardonnay due in part to their exposure to the coastal marine layer. Some of Santa Barbara County's wine industry pioneers grow and produce wines in this area.*

Babcock Vineyards / www.babcockwinery.com
    Babcock Vineyard – Chardonnay, Sauvignon Blanc, Pinot Grigio, Pinot Noir, Syrah
Casa Cassara Winery and Vineyard / www.ccwinery.com
    Casa Cassara Vineyard – Pinot Noir
Gypsy Canyon Winery / www.gypsycanyonwine.com
    Dona Marcelina's Vineyard – Misson
    Gypsy Canyon Vineyard (formerly Olivestone) – Pinot Noir, Pinot Gris
Lafond Winery & Vineyards / www.lafondwinery.com
    Lafond Vineyards, South 1997 – Pinot Noir, Syrah
Melville Vineyards/ Brewer-Clifton / www.melvillewinery.com
    Melville Vineyards – Chardonnay and Pinot Noir, Viognier and Syrah
    Kimberly Vineyard – Pinot Noir
Morovino (tasting room in Solvang) / www.morovino.com
    Morovino Vineyard – Pinot Grigio, Pinot Noir, Chardonnay, Syrah, Sangiovese, Barbera,
    Dolcetto and Grignolino
Richard Longoria Wines (tasting room in Los Olivos) / www.longoriawine.com

Fe Ciega Vineyard – Pinot Noir, Syrah and Merlot
Sanford Winery / www.sanfordwinery.com
Rancho la Rinconada – Chardonnay, Pinot Noir
Rancho el Jabali – Chardonnay, Pinot Noir
Rancho la Vina – Pinot Noir
Santa Barbara Winery (tasting room in Santa Barbara) / www.sbwinery.com
Lafond Vineyards, North 1972 – Pinot Noir, Chardonnay, Syrah, Sauvignon Blanc, White
Riesling, Zinfandel, Cabernet Sauvignon, Cabernet Franc
Sea Smoke Cellars / www.seasmokecellars.com
Sea Smoke Vineyard – Pinot Noir
Worx Cellars / www.wineatwork.com
Ampelos Vineyard – Pinot Noir, Syrah, Grenache, Viognier

## Santa Ynez Valley

*Santa Ynez Valley is considerably warmer than either the Santa Maria Valley or the Santa Rita Hills, enabling this region to excel in growing some of the best Syrahs in the United States, along with numerous other varietals. Flanked by the Santa Ynez Mountains to the south, and the San Rafael Mountains to the north, this well-established area maintains a pleasant, temperate climate.*

Andrew Murray Vineyards / www.andrewmurrayvineyards.com
Andrew Murray Vineyards – Syrah, Viognier, Roussanne, Grenache, Mourvedre
and Marsanne
Arthur Earl / www.santabarbara.com/winecountry/arthur
Beckman Vineyards / www.beckmenvineyards.com
Purisima Mountain Vineyard – Syrah, Marsanne, Rousanne, Grenache, Counoise
and Mourvedre
Bernat Vineyards & Winery / www.santabarbarawine.com
Bernat Vineyard – Syrah, Chardonnay, Merlot
Blackjack Ranch Vineyards & Winery / www.blackjackranch.com
Blackjack Ranch Vineyard – Syrah, Merlot, Cabernet Franc and Chardonnay
Brander Vineyard/ Domaine Santa Barbara / www.brander.com
Brander Vineyard – Sauvignon Blanc, Semillon, Chardonnay, Cabernet Sauvignon,
Cabernet Franc, Merlot
Bridlewood Winery / www.bridlewoodwinery.com
Bridlewood Vineyard – Syrah, Zinfandel
Buttonwood Farm Winery & Vineyard / www.buttonwoodwinery.com
Buttonwood Farm Vineyard – Sauvignon Blanc, Semillon, Marsanne, Merlot,
Cabernet Sauvignon, Cabernet Franc and Syrah

Carina Cellars / www.carinacellars.com
Consilience / www.consiliencewines.com
Curtis Winery / www.curtiswinery.com
 Ambassador's Vineyard – Syrah
 Crossroads Vineyard – Syrah, Grenache and Roussanne
Epiphany Cellars / www.epiphanycellars.com
Fess Parker Winery & Vineyard / www.fessparker.com
 Rodney's Vineyard – Syrah, Viognier, Chardonnay, Grenache, Petite Syrah
 Camp 4 Vineyard – Syrah, Viognier, Grenache, Roussane, Mourvedre
Firestone Vineyard / www.firestonewine.com
 Ambassador's Vineyard – Merlot, Riesling
 Brooks' Bench – Merlot, Cabernet Sauvignon
 Carranza Mesa – Merlot, Gewurztraminer, Chardonnay
 Crossroads – Chardonnay, Syrah
 Figueroa Terrace – Riesling, Cabernet Sauvignon, Sauvignon Blanc
 Jurassic Park – Sauvignon Blanc, Chenin Blanc, Cabernet Sauvignon
 Quati – Chardonnay, Cabernet Sauvignon, Merlot
 Zaca Station – Syrah
Foley Estates Vineyard & Winery/ Lincourt Vineyards / www.foleyestates.com
 La Cuesta Vineyard – Merlot and Cabernet Sauvignon
 Alamo Pintado Vineyard – Sauvignon Blanc and Cabernet Sauvignon
Gainey Vineyard / www.gaineyvineyard.com
 Los Robles Vineyard – Sauvignon Blanc, Semillon
 Meadowlark Vineyard – Cabernet Franc, Sauvignon Blanc, Semillon, Viognier
 Hillside Vineyard – Merlot, Cabernet Sauvignon, Syrah, Mourvedre, Grenache, Semillon and Riesling
Daniel Gehrs Wines / www.dgwines.com
Hitching Post Wines / www.hitchingpostwines.com
Kahn Winery / www.kahnwines.com
Kalyra/M. Brown / www.kalyrawinery.com
Koehler Winery / www.koehlerwinery.com
 Casa Blanca Vineyard – Cabernet Sauvignon, Chardonnay, Sauvignon Blanc, Riesling, Syrah and Sangiovese, Grenache and Viognier
Los Olivos Vintners – / www.santabarbara.com/winecountry/losolivos
Mosby Winery / www.mosbywines.com
 Mosby Vineyard – Gewurztraminer, Sangiovese, Nebbiolo, Barbera, Cortese, Dolcetto, Pinot Grigio, Teroldego
Rideau Vineyard / www.rideauvineyard.com
 Rideau Vineyard – Syrah, Viogner, Grenache Noir, Mourvedre, Roussanne

Royal Oaks Winery / www.royaloakswinery.com
    Royal Oaks Vineyards – Sauvignon Blanc, Merlot, Semillon
Rusack Vineyards / www.rusackvineyards.com
    Rusack Vineyard – Cabernet Sauvignon, Riesling, Muscat Canelli, Merlot, Cabernet Franc and Syrah
Sunstone Vineyards & Winery / www.sunstonewinery.com
    Sunstone Vineyard – Merlot, Cabernet Sauvignon, Syrah, Mourvedre
Zaca Mesa Winery / www.zacamesa.com
    Zaca Vineyards (Chapel, Fox-Run, Misty Ridge, Windmill) – Syrah, Chardonnay, Viognier, Grenache, Grenache Noir, Mourvedre, Roussane, Cinsaut

## MORE AREA TASTING ROOMS

**Los Olivos Tasting Room & Wine Shop**
**2905 Grand Ave., Los Olivos, CA 93441**
**www.losoliviswines.com**

Au Bon Climat – jim@abcqupe.com
Brophy Clark Cellars / www.brophyclarkcellars.com
Carhartt Cellars / www.carharttcellars.com
    Carhartt Vineyard – Syrah, Merlot
Cost de Oro Winery / www.costadeorowinery.com
DiBruno
Dierberg Vineyard – / www.dierbergvineyard.com
    Dierberg Crown Vineyard – Pinot Noir, Chardonnay
J. Kerr Wines – jkwines@msn.com
    JK Vineyard – Syrah
Kunin Wines
Lane Tanner Winery
Palmina / www.palminawines.com

**Los Olivos Wine & Spirits Emporium**
**2531 Grand Ave., Los Olivos, CA 93441**
**www.sbwines.com**

Benjamin Silver Wines / www.silverwine.com
Bonaccorsi Wine Company
Clos Pepe / www.clospepe.com
    Clos Pepe Vineyard – Chardonnay and Pinot Noir

Cold Heaven Cellars / www.coldheavencellars.com
Drew / www.drewwines.com
Fiddlehead Cellars / www.fiddleheadcellars.com
    Fiddlehead/Beringer Vineyard – Pinot Noir, Sauvignon Blanc
Flying Goat Cellars / www.flyinggoatcellars.com
Huber Winery
Kenneth Crawford Wines / www.kennethcrawford.com
Lane Tanner Winery
Loring Wine Company / www.loringwinecompany.com
Palmina / www.palminawines.com
Qupe Wine Cellars
Rozak Vintners
    Rozack Ranch Vineyard – Chardonnay, Pinot Noir
Stolpman / www.stolpmanvineyards.com
    Stolpman Vineyard – Cabernet Franc, Merlot, Cabernet Sauvignon, Sangiovese, Nebbiolo,
    Viognier and Syrah
Tantara Winery / www.tantarawinery.com
    Bien Nacido Vineyard G Block – Pinot Noir, Syrah
Vandale Vineyards / vanwine@silcom.com
    Vandale Vineyards – Sangiovese
Verdad Wines
Whitcraft Winery

**Santa Ynez Inn Wine Cellar**
**3631 Sagunto Street, Santa Ynez, CA 93460**

Au Bon Climat – jim@abcqupe.com
    Le Bon Climat Vineyard
Byron Vineyard & Winery / www.byronwines.com
    Byron Estate Vineyard – Pinot Noir and Chardonnay
Calzada Ridge Vineyard
    Calzada Ridge Vineyard – Viognier
Io / www.iowine.com
Qupe Wine Cellars
Westerly Vineyards / www.westerlyvineyards.com

**In Santa Barbara**

East Beach Wine Company / www.eastbeachwine.com
Jaffurs Wine Cellars / www.jaffurswine.com
Santa Barbara Winery / www.sbwinery.com
Stearns Wharf Vintners / www.stearnswharf.org
Margerum Wine Company/The Wine Cask Wine Store[201] / www.winecask.com

## ORGANIC VINEYARDS

All of Sanford's and Sunstone's vineyards are certified organic by the California Certified Organic Farmers (CCOF).[202]

Sanford Winery / www.sanfordwinery.com
    Rancho la Rinconada – Chardonnay, Pinot Noir
    Rancho el Jabali – Chardonnay, Pinot Noir
    Rancho la Vina – Pinot Noir
Sunstone Vineyards & Winery – / www.sunstonewinery.com
    Sunstone Vineyard – Merlot, Cabernet Sauvignon, Syrah, Mourvedre

---

[201] The Wine Cask Store has the most complete collection of Santa Barbara County wines anywhere.
[202] Organic Wine Labels have to adhere to the following guidelines:

'100% Organic Wine' on the main panel which includes the USDA seal is made from organically grown grapes and processed within the organic standards and with only the allowed organic materials from the national materials list, i.e., 100% organic ingredients and no sulfites added.

'Organic Wine' on the main panel which includes the USDA seal is made from organically grown grapes and processed within the organic standards and the allowed national materials list. A minimum of 95% ingredients must be organic with the remaining ingredients added only from the allowed national materials list, which includes the use of sulfur dioxide in wine up to 100 ppm (parts per million).

"Made from Organic Grapes," "Made from Organically grown Grapes," or "Organically Grown Grapes" in the ingredient list may not include the USDA seal. The wine must be made from organically grown grapes and processed within the BATF (Bureau of Alcohol, Tobacco & Firearms) guidelines but not within the allowed national materials list.

*The old rule about white wine with fish and red wine with meat made perfect sense in the days when white wines were light and fruity and red wines were tannic and weighty. But today, when most California Chardonnays are heavier and fuller-bodied than most California Pinot Noirs and even some Cabernets, color-coding does not always work.*[203]

Pairing food with wine can be learned with practice. Perhaps the first step is simply to begin paying attention to what wine you're drinking with what food. Take notes—especially when a wine really goes well with a particular entree or dish, and for that matter, when it doesn't.

## Basic Principles

The first decision that has to be made in pairing food and wine is in answering this question: Are we pairing food with a particular bottle of wine, or are we pairing wine with a particular entree or dish? There is a big difference in perspective, and the answer will probably come by considering what we want people to focus on. As Father Corbet Clark puts it, "Hungry people eating and drinking can concentrate only on so much at a time."[204] So, if we're pulling out that $35 bottle of Pinot Noir for dinner, we don't want to distract everyone with a 1-1/2" thick "prime grade" rib-eye steak from the grill. On second thought, wow...that sounds really good!

## Body

Next we need to pair the food with wine of equal body or weight. Remember the light, medium and full-bodied wine chart? (See Chapter 10) So really it's not that hard: a light-bodied wine with a light dish, a medium-bodied wine with a more substantial dish and a full-bodied wine with a heavy dish.[205] That's one reason why a Cabernet Sauvignon or a full-bodied Syrah[206] would probably be a better match for that rib-eye steak.[207]

Also, the cooking method has a lot to do with the weight and flavor of a particular dish:

---

[203] Harvey Steiman, editor at large. "Matching Wine with Food," Wine Spectator. http://www.winespectator.com/Wine/Wine_Basics/Wine_Basics_Template/0,1199,17,00.html

[204] Jeff Smith. *The Frugal Gourmet Cooks with Wine.* William Morrow and Company, New York: 1986. p. 404.

[205] More common sense from Harvey Steiman. "Hearty food needs a hearty wine, because it will make a lighter wine taste insipid. With lighter food, you have more leeway. Lighter wines will balance nicely, of course, but heartier wines will still show you all they have. Purists may complain that full-bodied wines "overwhelm" less hearty foods, but the truth is that anything but the blandest food still tastes fine after a sip of a heavyweight wine."

[206] A Syrah may vary in body and style depending on the microclimate in which it is grown and the style preference of the particular winemaker. One can't assume that a Syrah will be full-bodied, although it seems that most are.

[207] I remember reading somewhere that it is actually the fatty acids found in red meat that reduce the puckery sensation of the tannins in full-bodied reds, making them taste softer. Funny, how we always talk about a big red wine to go with that steak when we should be saying it the other way around.

- Steaming, poaching and boiling result in light dishes and impart minimal flavors.
- Sautéing produces a little more body and imparts slightly more flavor.
- Roasting, braising and baking results in a heavier dish, but enhances flavors in a gentle manner.
- Grilling adds an intense, smoky flavor that caramelizes or browns the food.
- Deep-frying obviously produces a heavy dish that coats the mouth.

## SIMILARITY AND CONTRAST

Third, we have to decide whether we are pairing for similarity or contrast. Most often we pair for similarity, but sometimes, with creamy or cheesy sauces that coat the tongue, we may want to pair for contrast by choosing a crisp, acidic wine to cleanse and refresh the palate.

Another reason to pair for contrast may relate to balancing the intensity of flavor. For instance, crisp light to medium-bodied wines allow the acidity of the wine to cut through the food. These "crisp" white wines are often paired with spicy hot dishes, like Thai or Chinese to "put the fire out" when our palates need a break.[208]

Don't rule out "off-dry" versions of Johannesburg Riesling or Gewürztraminer to match with rich foods. Sometimes they are just the ticket and provide the basis for redefining the meaning of "a balanced meal."[209]

## SAUCES

If the sauce is a prominent aspect of a particular dish, meaning you wouldn't think of serving the dish without the sauce, then pairing the wine to the sauce (instead of the main ingredient) becomes the priority.

Sauces change the flavor of foods; for instance, salmon on the grill with lemon, garlic and butter sure doesn't taste the same as poached salmon in a creamy dill sauce. "So, consider the balance of sweetness and tartness, the creaminess and the herbs in the sauce when thinking of a wine."[210] With various salsas, chutneys or relishes, choose a wine that matches the strongest flavor in the ingredients.

---

[208] The "heat" in most hot chilies comes from the natural oil found in the seeds. This helps us to understand why these more acidic wines, which help cleanse oil from the palate, can often make a good contrasting match.

[209] Even more Harvey..."At this point, let us interject a few words about sweetness. Some wine drinkers recoil at the thought of drinking an off-dry wine with dinner, insisting that any hint of sweetness in a wine destroys its ability to complement food. In practice, nothing can be further from the truth. How many Americans drink sweetened iced tea with dinner? Lemonade? Or sugary soft drinks? Why should wine be different? The secret is balance. So long as a wine balances its sugar with enough natural acidity, a match can work. This opens plenty of avenues for fans of German Rieslings, Vouvrays and white Zinfandel."

[210] Jeff Smith. The Frugal Gourmet Cooks with Wine. (William Morrow and Company, New York: 1986), pp. 404-405.

## ETHNICITY

Finally, consider pairing the ethnicity of the dish with the ethnicity of the wine. This doesn't mean we have to become experts on the wines of every nation of the world, or even of Western Europe for that matter. But, if I were looking for a red wine to go with spaghetti and meatballs, and I knew Sangiovese to be the dominant varietal used to make Chianti, I might decide to go with Sangiovese over Cabernet Sauvignon.

## PAIRING FOOD AND BEER

The same principles learned in appreciating wine and pairing wine with food applies also to beer. Recognition of the progression from light-bodied lagers[211] and medium-bodied pale ales[212] to full-bodied porters and stouts is fundamental to beer appreciation. In addition, we should learn to recognize various styles through sight, smell and taste.

Pairing beer with food through the common-sense approach related to body, similarity and contrast, sauces and ethnicity, works for me and I hope it works for you.

## PAIRING CHEESE AND WINE

| Soft Cheeses | Type of Wine |
| --- | --- |
| Mild | Light to medium-bodied whites |
| Strong/Aged | Full-bodied whites |
| Blue | Sweet or dessert whites |
| Ewe/Goat | Light to medium-bodied whites |
| Creamy | Champagne |

| Semi-Hard Cheeses | Type of Wine |
| --- | --- |
| Mild | Light to medium-bodied, whites or reds |
| Strong/Aged | Full-bodied whites or reds |
| Blue | Port, sweet or dessert whites or reds |

| Hard Cheeses | Type of Wine |
| --- | --- |
| Mild | Light to medium-bodied reds |
| Strong/Aged | Full-bodied reds |

[211] Bottom-fermenting yeasts produce lager-style beers, which are lighter, smoother and cleaner than most ales. Lagers include pilsners, bocks and a few other styles. American variations on the pilsner style, such as Budweiser, Coors and Miller, dominate the U.S. beer landscape. They are best consumed at cooler temperatures, although anything served colder than 38F will lose most of its flavor.
[212] Top-fermenting yeasts, which produce ales, include everything with ale in the name (pale ale, amber ale, etc.), porters, stouts and many specialty beers. They generally have a more robust taste, are more complex and are best consumed cool (50F or a bit warmer) rather than cold.

# DESCRIPTION OF CHEESES BY COUNTRY

## DENMARK

| Havarti | Soft | Mild, smooth, buttery. There are two types: dry rind or washed rind (has a richer flavor). |
|---|---|---|

## FRANCE

| Babybel | Soft | Mild French version of Dutch Edam, features colored wax coatings. |
|---|---|---|
| Bleu | Soft | Tangy, ripe, earthy and peppery. |
| Brie | Soft | Creamy, smooth, rich, buttery. |
| Camembert | Soft | Initially crumbly and soft, but gets creamier within 2-3 weeks). |
| Muenster | Soft | 8th Century monks from the French valley of Muenster first created this orange-rinded cheese. Mild to mellow. |
| Roquefort | Semi-Hard | Tingly, pungent taste. From milk of specially bred sheep. Creamy, thick and white on the inside with a thin burnt-orange skin. |

## GREAT BRITAIN

| Cheddar | Hard | Mild to sharp, tangy and robust. |
|---|---|---|
| Stilton | Semi-Hard | Crumbly yet moist. Sharp taste. There are two types of Stilton: Blue and White. |

## GREECE

| Feta | Soft | Salty, tangy, sharp flavor. Originally made with either ewe's milk or a mixture of ewe's and goat's milk, but is now being mass-produced with primarily cow's milk. The harder, crumbly version common in supermarkets is aged for up to 3 months. |
|---|---|---|

## ITALY

| Asiago | Hard | Sharp and primarily used for grating. |
|---|---|---|
| Gorgonzola | Soft | Stimulating, spicy blue cheese flavor Good served with pears. |
| Mozzarella | Soft | Spun-curd buffalo milk cheese. Mild, delicate, milky.[213] |
| Parmesan | Hard | Sharp, robust, yet savory. |
| Provolone | Semi-hard | Slightly tart and salty. |
| Romano | Hard | Similar, yet slightly richer than Parmesan, has a sharp, stimulating flavor. |

---

[213] This is quite different from the low-moisture mozzarella made in the US for the pizza industry.

## NETHERLANDS

| | | |
|---|---|---|
| Edam | Semi-hard | Mild and slightly salty with a nutty flavor. Available young or aged. |
| Gouda | Semi-hard | Mellow, rich caramel. Harder aged Goudas are also available with a smoked, strong, biting taste. |

## SWITZERLAND

| | | |
|---|---|---|
| Gruyere | Hard | Buttery and toasty. |

## UNITED STATES

| | | |
|---|---|---|
| American | Soft | Mild and delicate. Melts easily. |
| Brick | Semi-hard | Sweet, spicy and nutty. |
| Colby | Hard | Similar to cheddar. Mild to mellow, lightly sweet to sharp and tangy. |
| Colby Jack | Semi-hard | A combination of Monterey Jack and Colby cheeses. |
| Monterey Jack | Semi-hard | Mild, buttery, but zesty. Melts easily. Softer varieties are common in supermarkets. Pepper Jack Diced Jalapeños added to Monterey Jack. |
| Swiss | Semi-hard | Mild. Sweet, buttery taste. An American imitation of Swiss Emmental. |

According to professional coffeemakers, there are four fundamental aspects to brewing a good cup of coffee:

1) **Proportion.** Use 1-2 tablespoons of ground coffee for each six fluid ounces of water.[214]

2) **Grind.** The basic principle here is, the shorter the brewing process, the finer the grind. If your coffee tastes bitter, you may have ground the beans too fine for your machine. On the other hand, if your coffee tastes flat, they may have been ground too coarse. So, be sure and find out how fine a grind is recommended for the machine you're using to brew coffee.

3) **Water.** Use fresh cold water heated to just off a boil (195 to 205 F). Use filtered or bottled water if your tap water is not good or imparts a strong odor or taste, such as chlorine. If you are using tap water let it run a few seconds before filling your coffee pot. Do not use distilled or softened water.

4) **Freshness.** Use freshly ground coffee. Think of coffee as fresh produce. To keep coffee fresh, store it in an opaque, airtight container at room temperature. For the best results, coffee should be ground just before brewing. A burr or mill grinder is preferred over a blade grinder.

### Different Types of Roasted Coffee

Commercial coffee makers roast their coffee for a short period of time, about 8 or 9 minutes...it saves money...in labor, fuel, and only 10% to 14% of the weight is lost during roasting as compared to 18% to 25% for specialty roasters. Also, the soft, lesser-quality beans would burn up if left in the roaster longer. This is called Light or Half-City Roast. Commercial coffees typically use a blend of lower quality Arabica and Robusta beans. The flavor is light-bodied and somewhat sour, grassy and snappy.

Specialty roasters use a Medium or City Roast, where Arabica beans are roasted from 10 to 11 minutes. The color of the coffee becomes an even, light brown. The flavor is a bit sweeter than light roast—full body balanced by acid snap, aroma, and complexity.

Some specialty roasters roast their beans from 11 to 15 minutes, called Viennese or Full City Roast. The beans turn a rich chestnut brown with this type of roast, allowing the full flavor potential of the bean to be reached. The flavor is somewhat spicy; complexity is traded for rich chocolaty body and the sweetness is exchanged for aroma.

Dark Roasts include French, Italian and Espresso, where the color of the bean ranges from chocolate brown to nearly black. In these roasts, you mainly taste the smoky flavor of the roast, more than the bean. The roast period can go as high as 22 minutes.

**100% Kona Coffee.** With only 1,800 acres of coffee farms, Kona coffee is still handpicked and roasted in the tradition of generations of coffee plantation growers. When properly inspected, graded and roasted, the end result is a very delicate coffee with rich flavor and aroma

---

[214] I use two, but you can adjust the amount to suit your taste.

# Appendix F — General Serving Guidelines for Parties

| | |
|---|---|
| Hors d' oeuvres | 4oz per person |
| Tortilla Chips | 1-1/2oz per person |
| Potato Chips | 1oz per person |
| Bread | 1-1/2oz per person[215] |
| Meat | 4oz per person[216] |
| Potatoes or Salad | 4oz per person |
| Salad Dressing | 1oz per person |
| Vegetables | 4oz per person |
| Dessert | 4oz per person |
| Sheet Cake | 2" square per person |

## Beverages (per guest)

| | |
|---|---|
| White Wine/Champagne | 4oz |
| Champagne (for toasts) | 2oz[217] |
| Red Wine | 6oz |
| Beer | 12oz |
| Punch | 6oz |
| Coffee | 4oz |
| Soda/Water | 10-12oz |
| Ice | 1lb |

## Average Drink Consumption:
2 drinks per person for the first hour
1 drink per person each following hour

---

[215] Tortilla chips, potato chips and bread add up to a lot of carbohydrates. If you are going to serve all three, it would be best to scale back portions to equal 2 servings of "carbs" per person.

[216] If you are not serving Hors d' oeuvres or chips before the meal, you may want to increase the meat per person to 8oz. A good rule would be to plan for at least 20oz of food per person.

[2170] One 750ml bottle of champagne should serve 12 toasts.

## A FEW WORDS ABOUT CHAMPAGNE[218]

Strictly speaking, champagne means "French Champagne" coming from the Reims and Epernay districts east of Paris. California produces two types of Sparkling wine. The "Bulk Process" type is basically glorified soda pop. The other, usually labeled "Methode Champenoise," is produced using the traditional methods developed in the Champagne Region of France. It is well worth the price to buy a sparkling wine using the "Methode Champenoise."

It is also well worth a few dollars more to purchase a French Champagne. There is a significant difference in taste between the "fruit-driven" sparkling wines of California and the "yeast-driven" Champagnes produced in the chalky soils of France. The "doughy," "biscuity" bouquet on these champagnes is a treasure waiting to be discovered.

## HOW TO OPEN AND POUR CHAMPAGNE

Remove the outer foil wrap and untwist the wire cage. Keep your thumb on top of the bottle when untwisting the wire cage. Hold the bottle at a 45 degree angle and twist the bottle while firmly holding the cork. The cork should ease smoothly from the bottle with a delicate pop.

## SWEETNESS CHART FOR CHAMPAGNE

| French | American | Residual Sugar Description |
|---|---|---|
| Brut | Bone Dry | 0-1.5% bone dry to off-dry |
| Extra-Sec | Extra-Dry | 1.2-2% off-dry to medium dry |
| Sec | Dry | 1.7-3.5% medium dry |
| Demi-Sec | Semi-Dry | 3.5-5% sweet |
| Doux | Sweet | 5% plus dessert – like Spumante |

## A SPECIAL NOTE CONCERNING RESPONSIBLE HOSTING

One 12oz beer, one 4oz glass of wine[219] and 1-1/2oz shot of hard liquor (a jigger) all contain about the same amount of alcohol. A good rule of thumb is to limit consumption to 1 serving per hour per guest. Otherwise, you'd better not drink because you're going to be driving your guests home!

We've all heard the saying, "Don't drink and drive." Well here's another saying for the host: "Don't pour too fast, and monitor the alcohol consumption of your guests."

Moderation in all things—that's the key.

---

[218] Everything I know about champagne I learned from Patrick Coffield, instructor of the World of Wine class offered through the University of California Santa Barbara Recreation Center's Leisure Review programs. Patrick is a great teacher, his course is fun as well as informative and the class on champagne is my favorite.

[219] A 750 ml bottle contains approximately six 4oz servings. A 4oz serving is 1/2 cup—not a very big glass of wine. Most red wine glasses are so big that your guests may be offended by what appears to be such a small serving. So you may wish to pour a little more to start. Nevertheless, through the course of the evening, the average wine drinker should consume no more than about 12oz in the first two hours. Also, be sure to offer Hors d' oeuvres when serving alcohol to guests before the main courses are served.

# Index

*Notes from the Kitchen*

*Notes from the Kitchen*

*Notes from the Kitchen*

*Notes from the Kitchen*

*Notes from the Kitchen*